changing rooms

COMPLETE
HOME MAKEOVER

This book is published to accompany the television series *Changing Rooms,* which
is produced by Bazal (part of ENDEMOL Entertainment UK) for BBC TV.

Executive Producer: Linda Clifford

Published by BBC Worldwide Ltd
80 Wood Lane
London W12 0TT

First published 2001

Rooms designed by: Linda Barker, Laurence Llewelyn-Bowen,
Anna Ryder Richardson and Graham Wynne.
DIY Handyman: Andy Kane

ISBN 0 563 53781 7

Edited by Annabelle Grundy
Commissioning Editor: Nicky Copeland
Project Editor: Rachel Copus
Art Director: Lisa Pettibone
Book Designer: Kathryn Gammon

Set in Akzidenz Grotesk and DIN Mittelschrift Alternate
Printed and bound in France by Imprimerie Pollina s.a. - n° L82651
Colour origination by Imprimerie Pollina s.a.
Jacket printed by Imprimerie Pollina s.a.

In describing these projects, every care has been taken to recommend the safest ways
of working. The publishers and the authors cannot accept legal responsibility or liability for
accidents or damage arising from the use of any items mentioned, or in the carrying out
of the projects described in this book.

Safety warning
Protective equipment (goggles and mask) should be worn when using power tools,
such as drills, routers, jigsaws and sanders. It is also advisable to work outdoors and
wear protective equipment when sawing MDF and cane, or using spray cans.

COMPLETE HOME MAKEOVER

Simple ways to transform your home from
the Changing Rooms team

Contents

Introduction

When I first got involved with *Changing Rooms*, nearly five years ago, it all seemed like a bit of a laugh really. I was certainly very interested in interior design, especially the idea of making something out of nothing, but I didn't imagine for a moment that watching a programme about DIY would appeal to very many people. Since then I have had to eat my words many times over as the sack-loads of applications flood in. Hardly a day goes by without someone shouting at me in the street 'Oi, Carol, when are you going to come and do *my* room?'

One thing that never fails to impress me is the way in which people have taken on board the ideas behind the show. There's no denying that *Changing Rooms* has revolutionized the way we all think about our homes and how they reflect our own personal style. Gone are the days of wall-to-wall beige carpets and wood-chip wallpaper, now the whole country is busy constructing radiator covers and painting their walls in a rich variety of stylish and exciting colours.

Of course, by now, I know all of the designers inside out. I know Graham will always paint a room in cream and brown, given half a chance. Linda is in her own little Bohemian world (bless her!), Anna likes clean-cut, futuristic lines and, of course, Laurence does whatever Laurence fancies – the more outrageous the better, darling! And, before you ask, yes, I would let any of them into my house (as long as I was there to supervise!).

But if you have bought this book and are now wondering whether you have the confidence to attempt any of the projects in it, then my advice is just take a deep breath and have a go! It can always be changed. Don't be frightened of making a mistake, and have a little faith in yourself, because the end results will be well worth it. And remember, if I can do it … anybody can!

Making the most of this book

Transforming a room might seem like a daunting task, but don't panic – you've made the first move just by opening this book. Whether your room needs a floor-to-ceiling revamp or just a few fresh ideas, you'll find all the tips and guidance you need for success here.

Confused about colours? Turn to **Choose and change colour** to discover which shades blend best with your personality and lifestyle and how to put them together to suit your home. This section takes a detailed look at the four key palettes and reveals how to combine each one with other elements such as texture, accessories, lighting and furniture to create the mood you want.

Move on to **Manage that makeover** for some real down-to-earth advice on putting your own plans into action, from the nitty gritty of planning your budget and assessing your space to practical tips on painting, lighting and storage. The mysteries of that vital designer's tool, the mood board, are blown away, so that you'll soon be compiling, understanding and using your own board to bring your ideas to life. Then, follow the *Changing Rooms* designers through some real-life transformations, seeing how they deal with everyday problems and work within tight budgets to turn clutter and confusion into style and serenity. You'll pick up in-depth information and plenty of inspiration from their creative solutions for challenging spaces ranging from living and dining areas to bedrooms for kids and grown-ups and even a kitchen.

All this is sure to leave you brimming with enthusiasm and eager to get started on your own projects, so you'll be keen

to **Try this at home**. In this section you'll find over 60 practical ideas to tackle yourself, all with easy to follow step-by-step instructions that will help you achieve fabulous results, even if you've never attempted to make anything before. The projects cover all aspects of decorating and furnishing a room, from simple suggestions for brightening up cushions or windows to dramatic wall and floor-treatments. Even building your own furniture need not be as alarming as you might think. Whether it's basic shelving, storage boxes or something more ambitious, such as a pelmet, wardrobe or radiator cover, there are guidelines here to help you through, plus invaluable safety information. Each project starts with a list of all the equipment you'll need, and there are clear instructions and photographs to make sure you don't go wrong.

These pages will give you the inspiration and know-how to change your surroundings. All you need to supply is your own energy and imagination. Enjoy!

Meet the team

Linda Barker

Before establishing herself as a professional interior designer, Linda was originally a fine artist. As well as making regular appearances on *Changing Rooms*, Linda co-presents her own show, *House Invaders*, for the BBC. In addition to her television work Linda undertakes private commissions and writes articles for design magazines, notably the *Saturday Telegraph Magazine*, where she has a regular interiors column. She has also written a number of books including her most recent titles, *Jazz up your Junk* and *Trade Secrets*. Her corporate clients include Crest Homes, and she has her own range of wallcoverings with Crown.

Andy Kane

A crucial member of the *Changing Rooms* team, 'Handy' Andy has worked as a carpenter and joiner ever since he left school and gained his City and Guilds qualifications. After joining *Changing Rooms*, he soon rose to stardom and has since worked on a number of other television series, including the BBC Daytime series *Change That*, where Andy was responsible for bringing the designers' ideas to life.

Laurence Llewelyn-Bowen

Originally a fine artist, Laurence has since turned his attention to interior design and is a frequent contributor to *Changing Rooms*. He also has his own popular series, *Fantasy Rooms,* and *Home Front*, which he co-presents with Diarmuid Gavin. Off-screen, Laurence's work has featured in a number of interior design magazines, including *Homes and Ideas* and the *Express on Saturday* and *Sunday*, and he has undertaken commissions at a variety of locations including the Opera Terrace at Covent Garden. He recently released his book, *Display*.

Anna Ryder Richardson

As well as making regular appearances on *Changing Rooms*, Anna has presented and designed for a number of BBC television series including *House Invaders*, *Girls on Top*, *All the Right Moves*, *Whose House* and *Change That*. She also writes a weekly feature for the *Sun* and runs her own business, $A^2 2000$.

Graham Wynne

Originally a theatre designer, Graham is an established member of the *Changing Rooms* team and has also made regular appearances on *Change That*, *Party of a Lifetime* and *The Great House Challenge*. In addition to his television work, Graham has worked as a designer and stylist for a variety of corporate clients, including Harvey Nichols and Selfridges, and has written articles for a number of design magazines including BBC *Good Homes*, *Period Living* and *Traditional Homes*.

Choose
& change
colour

Colour is undeniably the most important element of a
room scheme, and often presents the biggest problem.
The right choices can make a room sing, so don't back
towards that tin of magnolia. With a few designers' hints,
colour sense and confidence are well within your grasp.

First things first

Colour is one of the most exciting aspects of decorating. Recent trends have broken almost every rule and any shade is acceptable today. As there are now no boundaries, selecting the right colours can seem a daunting task. The guidelines below should help you make choices that will enhance your home.

Know yourself

You probably already have some ideas about the shades you love or loathe and your own instincts are the best place to start. Whether you are drawn to faded denim, rich purple damask or a vibrant fuchsia lipstick, this is your clue. Assemble items from all over your home that you love for their colour. These may be scarves, plates, soaps or postcards – anything goes at this stage. Study books and magazines too for pictures that strike a chord. Add to, reject and play around with the assortment until you begin to recognize the colour combinations that appeal. Remember, there's no one to please except yourself and the others in your home, and there are no strict rules. The shade you choose, how much of it you use, what you combine it with and the way the light hits it are the factors that really determine its effect.

Once you have established the colours you like, test them out using crayons, watercolours or whatever is to hand. Add a little white to tubes of colour to lighten a shade, or deepen a tone with a touch of a complementary one. When the colours are blended to perfection, take a look at the paint charts. Match a paint tone with an area of colour and the choice of shade will start to become more manageable. Bear in mind that your chosen colour will have far more

below Blue and white is a classic and versatile colour combination that has great appeal. Teamed with cream in a bedroom it is both fresh and restful.

above Fuchsia pink lies directly opposite lime green on the colour wheel, guaranteeing an unnervingly brilliant contrast. A relatively small amount of fuchsia prevents the lime from dominating the whole space.

impact on four walls than on a small sample, so find the best match and then take it down a couple of notches.

Suit the situation

Having identified the colours you want to live with, you should bear in mind that there are circumstances where certain choices will disappoint. It's very easy to fall in love with the vibrant blues, oranges and turquoises you might see on holiday in the Mediterranean, but these bright colours will not work unless they are saturated by strong sunlight. A clear yellow in a north-facing room with little daylight can appear drab. (See Manage that makeover, page 66.) The muddier the

colour you choose the better it will suit the cool northern light in the UK, so lavender, sage or ochre will be more successful than bright canary yellow, emerald or cobalt blue.

Tricks of the light

Light, both natural and artificial, will have all kinds of effects on colour and it is essential to be aware of these before you commit yourself. Think about the times of day when you will be using the room. A dining room, for example, may have very poor natural light but this may not matter if you use it mainly in the evenings, and light it with candles. Spend some time watching to see when, and how much, light comes into your room and how it moves around. When you choose your shade, buy a small sample pot first. Apply the entire contents to a big sheet of cardboard or MDF. Leave this propped in your room, remembering to move it around to different corners and study it in all lights over at least a week. If you still love the colour, then it is probably the right shade for you.

Colour companions

Finding the right colour for your walls is the first hurdle, but no scheme will work with just a single shade. Combining colours can be problematic, but there is a device, the colour wheel, to help. This is separated into six basic shades: red, blue and yellow (primaries) and violet, orange and green (secondaries). Colours lying between, like turquoise, which is a mix of blue and green, or

crimson, made from red and violet, are tertiaries. A twelve-colour wheel is thus built up, each colour blending into its neighbours.

Harmonizing colours lie next to each other, and produce a soft

scheme where the eye passes easily from one shade to the other. Complementary colours are those that lie opposite each other and are naturally discordant. When handled correctly, a flash of a complementary colour creates a brilliantly vibrant effect that can lift a colour scheme and prevent one shade from dominating all the others.

Grand illusions

Colour is a subtle tool, useful for hiding or highlighting aspects of your room. Use cool colours containing lots of blue to make walls appear to

left Despite containing at least six different shades, the overall effect here is mellow because no single tone stands out. Hot colours are usually thought to be stimulating, but used in a harmonizing way, the opposite is true.

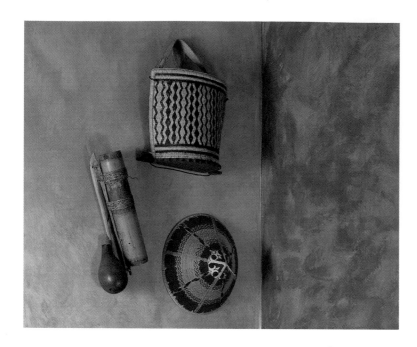

recede. Conversely, warm tones with plenty of red will seem to bring them closer together and can make a stark room more inviting. Applied decoration such as colour-washing or stencilling adds another layer to the wall colour, giving the impression of looking through to the solid colour

left Colour-washing creates a broken effect, allowing you to use shades that could otherwise seem too strong.
below The darkness of this unusual olive-green is countered by the layering on top of gleaming copper leaf, adding contrast and extra depth.

behind. Techniques like these allow you to use dark, powerful colours in the smallest of spaces such as bathrooms and hallways. As long as they are somehow broken up they will not necessarily make the room seem smaller.

A pale colour will make a low ceiling appear higher, while a lofty ceiling can be visually lowered by either using a darker colour than the one on the walls or continuing its colour down to picture-rail height. Awkwardly angled walls and sloping ceilings can be disguised by painting them the same unifying colour. Deflect attention from an ugly corner by drawing the eye to a bright patch of colour elsewhere, or make a wonderful display area by painting one wall a completely different shade from the rest. Use dado or picture rails to separate different colours and finishes.

Colour can also be used to unify the separate spaces within your home. If you want to make your house feel bigger inside, choose pale colours that are in sympathy with one another so that there is a feeling of continuity from one room to the next. Strong contrasts such as a fiery red room leading to a rich forest-green one will create a dramatic and exciting atmosphere.

below A sloping ceiling can be disguised by painting it the same colour as the walls, thus blending the two surfaces and minimizing the angles.

Finding the right colours for a room can be a daunting task, because there is literally an infinite number of choices and it can all seem overly complicated. Don't be intimidated! Below, a few designers' terms are demystified:

Accent colours Sharp colours chosen to lift a scheme, eg, hot pink cushions and candles in a mainly cream and navy living room. Highlights is another term for accent colours.

Base colour The colour, usually the wall shade, used in the greatest proportion. It is often chosen as the canvas for introducing contrasts, accents or colours that complement each other.

Clashing colours These create an extreme effect, vibrating in front of you and continuing to resonate when you close your eyes. Juxtapositioning is all-important here, so go for maximum impact.

Cold colours These contain a lot of blue. Cool greys for example, might make you shiver as you put them on the wall, but a grey tone containing a lot of magenta would have quite a different character. (See Warm colours)

Contrasting colours These give a room heart-stopping impact, and never come from the same family. Think of burnt-orange cushions placed against a cool blue background.

Dominant colour This is not always the colour used in the greatest proportion but it is the one that stands out from the rest.

Family of colours This applies to colours that are in some way related. For example, the blue family includes greeny tones at one end and purples at the other. Browns stretch from coffee and taupe (brownish-grey) to shades of orange and red.

Warm colours These contain a lot of magenta. Even blues can fall into this category, so don't be deterred from using them because you feel they could look cold. (See Cold colours)

Toning colours These are colours that share the same depth of tone, such as a strong yellow and strong blue. They are not necessarily from the same family, but they each contain the same amount of red or blue and none overpowers the others.

Natural order

It is easy to dismiss Naturals as not being proper colours, but in fact they are as valid as red or blue, with a certain intensity of their own. Natural colours conjure up savoury images of the simple good things of life: farmhouse cheeses and wholemeal bread. You can also draw abundant inspiration from the outdoor world, be it from limestone and granite, sycamore and maple trees or fields of barley and wheat. Natural cottons, canvases and linens are at the heart of the clean, bleached look of Scandinavian interiors. The Natural palette appeals to the sense of touch almost as strongly as it does to sight. Think of the contrast between rough, undyed calico and a stone table. In fact, in this part of the spectrum texture is nearly as important as the colours themselves.

Naturals are a demanding choice in the home, requiring great discipline as no single object should unsettle the total picture, even if this means living without some favourite things. These are colours for people who value the spiritual as well as the material. They demand that you choose every possession with care, but they reward you with calm and serenity.

below The Natural palette is made up of infinite tones, while contrasting textures add an entirely new dimension.

Using Naturals

Naturals work best in rooms with good light, so are ideal for the cool northern light of the UK. Muted blends of woods, white and cream make relaxing backdrops for living, the idea being that colours should work in harmony rather than fight each other for attention. You also have the option of introducing flashes of a more definite colour here and there – perhaps with a change of a tablecloth or throw – according to your mood or the time of year. The Natural palette is an easy way of decorating. All whites, whether they are tinged with blue,

pink, yellow or grey, work well together. As they incorporate shades of other colours they change according to what they are near. The only exception to this is brilliant white, which can be surprisingly intrusive and should be used with care. Any reasonably sized space, from a modern loft-style apartment to a period house, looks great with Naturals. This does not mean that naturals have no place in smaller homes, but it would be difficult to give them much impact in a tiny cottage with dark-beamed ceilings. What counts are the proportions of the room, the light within it and your own confidence to work with a range of colours that might not look that special on their own.

Layers of meaning

Although they appear to be the simplest and least contrived of interiors, it takes the greatest skill to do a Natural room well. The key to using this palette successfully is to embrace the idea of layering textures and subtle colours. Natural shades are not always strong enough to work just as flat colour and can look very dull, so they need the second dimension of surface variation to bring them to life. Texture, more than colour, can be the driving force. It is not simply a question of picking a suitable shade for the walls, but of deciding whether to choose a rough plaster or Italian stucco surface, or even fabric-swathed walls. Done cleverly, Naturals are breathtakingly beautiful and also very sensual, delighting fingertips as much as eyes. Build up the effect, starting with a wall treatment that combines matt and gloss surfaces. Then introduce fur, linen, silk, stone, twigs and anything else that makes your fingertips tingle. The key to using texture lies in contrast: velvet will appear at its most sensuous placed next to cool hard glass or steel. A coarse, rough fabric will bring out the patina of polished wood.

Clear vision

Naturals don't have to mean minimalism, but they do require purism and simplicity. Having said that, it can be liberating to scale down belongings to the few that really matter and work well. Each ingredient, be it floor, furniture or even flowers, must hold its

below For the Natural palette to work successfully ornaments must be carefully chosen, with the emphasis on a few perfect items.

own in the total scheme, but not overwhelm it. For this reason accent colours are more likely to be chocolate brown or iron grey than acid green or shocking pink. The aim, if possible, is to pare down your belongings so that the eye is drawn to one or two objects of pure beauty – perhaps a vase you love, a collection of simple white china, some gleaming glass or a bowl of iridescent shells. Naturals can help you produce an interior that is

uncluttered and serene, with an almost Zen-like beauty. Take your inspiration from Japanese homes, where interiors are of the utmost simplicity, but include one object of beauty on which to meditate: perhaps a single glorious flower or perfect piece of pottery. In Western society this is the most contemporary of interior schemes, although the philosophy behind it is thousands of years old and is familiar throughout

above Clean, simple lines ensure that furniture is in harmony with the understated Natural tones.

the East. Followers of Feng Shui will recognize some of the references as it is believed that energy can flow more freely in this kind of space, allowing life to be more creative and fulfilling. It might not be practical to turn your entire home over to this style of decoration immediately, but it could benefit from at least one calm, inviting and sensual space.

Stone story

Shades from buttermilk through café au lait to bitter chocolate may not at first seem very inspiring, but the variations of no-colour Naturals are as subtle, numerous and addictive as other more brilliant palettes. They are the colours of stone, wood, bare earth and an autumn landscape. Their dynamism comes into play as they are juxtaposed with each other. They are wonderfully easy to work with because you can layer so many visual and textural ingredients into a room, confident that harmony will reign and no single element will shout for attention. These colours work best in a generously proportioned room with good natural light to bring out the myriad shades and surfaces.

Contrasting textures are the core of a no-colour Natural room. Source adventurously for the soft, hard, shiny and matt elements. These could be anything from a mirrored chimney breast and fur sofa-throws to African-inspired pots, a splintery wooden Buddha or a distressed Indian coffee-table. Also look for ways of leading the eye through the room to the walls: wrought-iron furniture and

accessories are excellent for achieving this as they have an almost transparent quality.

One or two pieces of strong colour are important to anchor the other shades, but to introduce anything vivid would disturb the tranquil atmosphere. Chocolate brown is the best solution, strong enough to give definition yet in keeping with the neutral theme. It can be successfully added in fairly large quantities. A studded leather chair or suede

opposite While colour in this room is muted, textures range from stone to fur, and glass to wood, building a rich and diverse scheme.
below Paler Naturals need to be anchored by splashes of a stronger colour, such as chocolate brown or black, which, although in the same family, bring some backbone to the total picture.

cushions, for example, would add weight to the scheme and also accentuate the textural theme. Even the smallest splash of a more definite colour would distract attention from the layers of texture.

Shades of grey

Grey is not a colour that people are naturally drawn to. It can have overtones of coldness and austerity. Yet, as is often demonstrated in nature, grey can also be quite beautiful. What makes it work so well in the natural world is that it is often juxtaposed with warmer shades, like black streaking the grey feathers of a sea bird, or red and gold flecks on grey pebbles on the shore. Take your cue from this when using it to decorate your home. Most greys contain quite a lot of magenta, making them warmer than you might

first think, and you can bring this out by choosing warm colours as your accent shades. Another advantage of grey is its versatility. It can become a backdrop for whatever you want to impose on a room – maybe a cool look designed around many layers of blue, or a minimalist's delight when teamed with black. Alternatively you could take the more modern route, painting three walls in soft dove for example, and one in chocolate brown or mauve for an exciting contrast.

Grey must have a room with good light otherwise it can look very stark and unwelcoming. If yours is not too well lit, but you have set your heart on this colour scheme, look for a way to boost the light artificially, perhaps with well-positioned spotlights. Paint can seem to change colour according to how the light hits it, and when using grey you might find one wall actually looks more like blue. It is a good idea to choose off-white for the woodwork and ceiling, as brilliant white will probably make grey look too harsh.

An accent shade is necessary to prevent the scheme looking too cold. Using hot colours such as oranges, ochres and even a touch of red is one way of warming up cool base shades. Bright cobalt blue is also a clever choice. It is the perfect foil for grey as both colours come from the same family. It will also bring a seaside flavour to the room. Use cobalt in a slightly textured paint finish so that it doesn't stand out too strongly. By keeping all the accent colours soft and hazy you will accentuate the peaceful nature of the room.

opposite Grey might not seem an obvious choice for a room, but blended with warm wood and gentle sandy shades, it has a clean, natural appeal. **below** Adding tones of linen and sand can warm a cool blue. The look is still fresh, and reminiscent of the sea.

In a grey-based scheme texture is again an important facet, adding a sensual dimension to a living space and emphasizing that decorating is about more than just paint colours. As textural layers are built up, grey will lose its cold edge and become mellow. The paint in the pot might look quite daunting and as chilly as the North Sea, but it may still be an excellent base for unifying other elements. It is important to remember that you must look at all the components of a room in relation to each other before you can judge properly whether a colour is working well.

Dreamy cream

Naturals create a calm, restful atmosphere, a cocoon from the outside world. Cream is the warmest of the natural shades, which is one reason why it remains perennially popular. Its attraction also lies in its versatility. Cream can work with just about any colour imaginable and act as a base for stronger tones. It also creates a wonderful mood of understated elegance, with a classic appeal that few other colours can emulate.

Strong textural interest is essential if you want to avoid an old-fashioned magnolia scheme. A paint finish will add visual interest, or rough-plastered walls will give more depth to the colour. Another option which makes a strong statement is to line the walls with fabric like dustsheets (see page

right Distressed furniture is ideal for a Natural scheme, because its surface detail becomes the focus of interest. Old glass bottles and pebbles can add to a seashore theme.

opposite Dashes of a substantial colour, like aubergine, act as a foil, giving definition and impact to a room lined in all-enveloping cream.

144, Fabric-lined walls) to give texture as well as all-round colour. If you also line the ceiling, you will create a marquee effect. The wrapping theme can be continued by swathing furniture in fabric too.

Enveloping everything in creamy colour is far more seductive than having solid items of furniture. Good lighting is crucial to a heavily textured theme like this. A simple overhead light would flatten and deaden the effect, so look for lighting to accentuate the design.

Having created a soft cocoon of natural shades, you need to add an accent colour to give the scheme some weight. Aubergine is perfect as

above Lighting can make or break a highly textured scheme. These uplighters throw out dramatic beams of light, drawing attention to the fabric-lined walls.

it punctuates all the creaminess, giving the room direction, but is about as far as you should push the Natural palette. Other options would be chocolate brown, pigeon grey or slate. Take care not to introduce too many colours, which could detract from the impact of the Naturals.

There in black and white

Although the extremes of black and white might seem out of place in this palette, both are vital foils that bring out the subtleties of the Naturals. A stone-inspired scheme could fall into

the trap of looking overly muted, restrained and lacking in clarity. Combat this by using pure white instead of cream on woodwork and skirting boards, and keep the skirtings as deep as possible so that they almost frame the walls. White will lift all the other colours and give definition to the entire room. Teamed with Naturals, it is a surprisingly strong colour that can be used in small but effective ways, such as on picture frames or in a vase of flowers, to bring a refreshing edge to a neutral room.

Black can play a similar role. A small touch, even if it is only a fire surround, has a graphic quality that draws attention to other shades. You don't need very much to make an impact. Curtain poles, picture frames or occasional pieces of furniture are ideal for introducing it into a scheme. Use both black and white sparingly with Naturals as they should not dominate.

Surrounding style

If you opt for the Natural approach you need never buy a carpet again. Sanded floorboards which are then varnished, bleached or limed make the perfect foil for natural shades. Parquet flooring is a more sophisticated option that is also an ideal base for this range of colours. Natural floor coverings like jute, sisal, coir and seagrass would blend into the mood and add more surface interest, too. Furniture can be as battered or as beautiful as you want. A distressed finish will accentuate
the textural qualities of the room. However, cheap and cheerful is not essential as contemporary designers are producing wonderful sculptural pieces in woods and veneers that could take centre stage anywhere. On the other hand, you could renovate a junk-shop table yourself and place the most perfect glass vase of lemons or a wicker basket of shiny pebbles on it.

Finishing touches

Windows can be dressed with simple wooden shutters, billowing calico, delicate lace panels or swathes of soft muslin. The choice you make should reflect the wall surfaces, flooring and general ambience of the room. It will also depend on whether you are trying to frame a perfect view or block out the sounds and sights of the street. Accessorize with a few well-chosen items like a beautiful bowl or box, and with objects in tune with the natural inspiration of these colours: a large fossil ammonite with its organic curving form and ridged stony surface, or simple twigs, shells and pebbles gathered outdoors.

below A group of carefully chosen pieces adds further elements of contrast and organic form to the Natural story. The vivid splash of perfect flowers punctuates pale colour.

Pastel potential

Imagine taking a delicious colour like a brilliant blue or post-box red, and then pouring milk into it so that it becomes dense and opaque. Modern Pastels are the colours of sugared almonds, making you think of pistachio ice cream and strawberry tarts. They have far more strength than the 'Hints of…' pale shades that used to dominate the paint charts, and create a hazy effect, like looking through fine muslin, which gives the impression that walls are receding. This makes Pastels the perfect choice for those dingy spaces where you want to create a feeling of energy and light. They also engender a peaceful atmosphere, ideal for people with busy lives who want to return to spaces that soothe them.

Pastels do not shout and clash. Instead they wash over you, leaving you with a sense of tranquillity. They don't demand the purist approach of the Naturals, nor the courage of the Vivids, so they are an excellent halfway house. They have a classic appeal that will always have a place in our lives, showing off a fine room to perfection by creating an atmosphere of calm.

below A Pastel scheme opens up space, accentuates light and seamlessly draws you from one area to the next. Gentle greens love the honey tones of natural wood.

Using Pastels

The beauty of Pastels is that they are very easy to live with, and are suitable for any room. Traditionally popular for bedrooms and bathrooms, today they have relevance throughout the house. For instance, they are ideal for living spaces where you want to merge one area into another and have a sense of continuity as you look through doors into adjacent rooms. They are also perfect if you want to change your furnishings according to the seasons: loose covers, curtains, cushions and accessories can all be replaced with another set, yet the backdrop remains the same.

Light and shade

To do themselves justice Pastels need good light, otherwise they can fade away into insignificance, or look stark and cold. This is particularly true of the blue family. If windows are small and the natural light is poor, you should consider introducing extra artificial light, especially for the evenings. Halogen lighting is best as it brings out warmth and shows the true nature of colours. Without good lighting a pale colour scheme will have only a quarter of its impact, so make sure you're happy with the way it will be lit before you start painting. Remember, natural light can change, even within a single room, to the extent that two walls painted the same shade can appear to be totally different colours.

Pep it up

Because Pastels create a plain background there is a danger that they could look boring. The secret is to break up expanses of space and create interest for the eye. In an average-sized room with good light other accent colours will bring Pastels to life. Imagine, for example, pale lilac walls. Now add a burnt-orange sofa and other hot-coloured accessories. The lilac will take on a new dynamism with such strong companions.

below A variety of shades will inject energy and keep Pastels looking lively. The addition of silver here ensures a contemporary look in this room.

In a smaller space it is vital to create character, breaking up plain walls that could look bland. Pictures are one way of doing this, and applied decoration is another option. Wide, horizontal stripes of flat colour painted around the walls will play a visual trick, making the space seem bigger than it really is. A much warmer shade, say a denim blue, can be used to punctuate a pale tone of ice blue. You can then colour-wash the lower third of the walls by dragging the warmer shade down over the pale one to create more interest (see page 126).

Another way to introduce a touch of excitement and give more edge to a colour scheme is to paint one wall a slightly stronger shade from the same Pastel family, such as a smoky blue against three walls of lilac. If you have a small room with limited natural light, and feel you have no choice but to use a muted Pastel shade, this approach could satisfy any longings for more intense colour. Tonal combinations are highly effective and the colours won't take your breath away as you put them on the wall. Blocks of colour on walls are the latest trend in interiors, fast replacing colour-washing, stencilling, dragging and the like, and Pastels are perfect for experimenting in this way.

If a room has a dual function, such as a living-cum-dining room, you can use Pastel colours and applied decoration to distinguish between the two areas. For example, choose stripes for one end of the room and squares for the other; that way the two ends can be unified in both

colour and geometry while still retaining their own characters. Bear in mind that you don't have to use the decoration at the same height each time; it is quite OK to bring the eye towards dado level in one area and up to the coving in another. This will actually emphasize the height and proportions of a room.

Since there is so much scope in Pastels, texture will play a smaller part

above Pastels are an ideal background for some striking applied decoration. The unexpected continuation of this stripe over furniture adds further visual interest.

than in other colour families. However, the combination of rough and smooth does have relevance to the Pastel palette. Meanly proportioned rooms, the obvious places for these colours, benefit from textural contrasts that distract attention from the overall space and focus it on to specific items. With Pastels you can also be braver about using pattern, and even use more than one without fear of them clashing wildly. Take pattern up a notch – go that bit bolder than you usually dare.

Combining colours

Pastels are simple colours to play around with – you can combine them to your heart's content. There is no need to be restricted to numbers – you could use five or six of these shades in a room and get away with it because they are all light tones that are easy on the eye. You could choose one colour for the walls, another for the skirting board, a third for the upholstery, a fourth for the curtains and yet another for key accessories.

You might feel a bit nervous about using certain Pastels such as pink and lilac, which could remind you of little girls' bedrooms. or ice blue, with its chilly overtones. Some of these shades are not natural choices. However, it's what you complement them with, and how they are lit, that will make all the difference.

Perfect pink

The idea of a pink room, with its sugary associations, is one that has

above A fresh, airy look could appear chill and uninviting in the absence of natural light. The success of the Pastel scheme, particularly the blue family, depends on good lighting.

right Pastel pink can look surprisingly sophisticated. Shocking pink is a clever choice of accent colour, countering the powerful effect of the main shade.

many people reaching for the smelling salts. Yet pink has gradually crept into contemporary interiors, starting in the 1980s when many commercial designs exploited Italian-style plaster pink. The 1990s continued the trend with increasingly chic ways of combining pink with other colours – grey, black, cream

above Large diamonds and an intentionally imperfect finish add tonal variation, interest and movement, preventing the wall colour from dominating the room.

above right Flamboyant accessories, like this ornate silver-framed mirror, suit the exuberance of a predominantly pink room.

and green, for example – to achieve numerous looks. Bedrooms and bathrooms are the obvious places to try it out, but in fact it has great relevance as a living-room or dining-room colour because it shares many of the same qualities as cream – it is warm, welcoming and enveloping.

Pink is also surprisingly versatile and can work as well in a small, dark room as in a large, airy one. It doesn't demand the same quantity of light as blues and greys – in fact candlelight alone can give it a fabulously seductive look. When you move away from baby pinks into the denser shades you realize it is actually a very sexy colour. When pink works well there is nothing like it for creating a soft and sensual atmosphere. It is

also ideal for a period house as it has a long and influential connection with country-house decoration. Look through any of the historical paint ranges now available and you will find muddy shades of pink that suit Britain's northern light perfectly.

For walls, pink works better as a textured surface than as a flat colour. Try a rough plaster or colour-washed look with another warm shade, like cream, to break up the pinkness. Soft green is another excellent ally in this respect, as it is pretty without being twee. Not all Pastels would work so well. You need a colour with a little punch that will not be submerged by a pink base. Accent colours also need to be able to hold their own against pink. If you have used a sugar pink on the walls you could try teaming it with a shocking pink or coral for even more zing. Black is a clever choice as it brings definition to a room, although you might find it too stark. Charcoal grey is a brilliant in-between shade – powerful enough to take on pink yet not so strong that it tires the eyes. It gives sophistication to a scheme and saves it from becoming too feminine.

Simplicity is the key to keeping a pink room chic, so don't introduce too many other colours as this could make the result rather cloying and sickly. A slightly distressed finish on furniture, echoing a textural theme on the walls, is ideal and the colours of the floor, window treatments and accessories should all accentuate the mood of restfulness. Cream is a good choice, as are naturals.

Love lilac

Like pink, lilac has been seen as overtly feminine and so has been largely ignored in decorating in recent years. Happily, people are now recognizing what a versatile colour it is. Teamed with black, it seems chic and somehow French, like something you would see in a Parisian apartment. Adding silver to the scheme creates a sophisticated and dynamic combination, very different from the chintzy way lilac is often used with pale greens, yellows and pinks.

Ice-blue heaven

Ice blue sits comfortably with many other colours: cream if you want to warm it up, white for a really cool atmosphere, grey to echo the

seashore, or black for a sharper edge. Bear in mind that you must have good light to use blues and mauves successfully. Use other materials to warm them up. For example, a natural wooden floor can be glazed in a sandy shade to lighten it. Natural wooden shutters are ideal at the windows. If you choose soft, textured fabrics such as linen, calico and muslin to layer the scheme, none of the colours will jar and should ultimately create a calming, liberating space. Metallic silver, the fashionable choice of the moment, is fabulously

below Lilac is currently enjoying a comeback, producing a calmly understated modern look. The pinky tones lend warmth to the cooler, bluer ones.

exciting with blues of all descriptions. For a softer look, another choice would be to team pale blue with other sugary shades such as pale greens, pinks and yellows. If you want to bring in more impact, stronger colours like burnt orange, blueberry or blackcurrant can be used to draw the eye.

Lemon sorbet

Shades of yellow are usually felt to be uplifting, cheerful and inspirational and, despite their softer edge, those falling into the Pastel palette are no exceptions. Welcoming tones from buttermilk to banana are perfect for entrances, hallways and landings as well as kitchens and living rooms.

While shades of lemon veering towards green can show off a sunny space to its optimum, tones with more red in them are also a good choice if you want to warm a room, such as a windowless bathroom that lacks natural daylight. White woodwork rather than cream will give definition, preventing the overall effect from becoming too cloying.

Pastel yellows are happiest teamed with close associates, so for accent colours look to fresh greens to create a positive mood. Mellow apricot or peach will produce a softer, more relaxing feel. This combination comes into its own in dining rooms in particular, as it has the versatility to

work either in daylight or with more subdued lighting like candles. Yellows tend to fight with pale blues and pinks, but work well with naturals like grey, cream and stone so experiment with accessories like linen fabrics, cobbles, rope and weathered wood. This will also give the option of adding hints of darker accents such as slate grey or brown which will contrast but not jar.

Green and pleasant

The actors' 'greenroom' is so called because of the soothing effect its décor is supposed to have on pent-up pre-performance nerves. As green is a combination of blue and yellow, tones of Pastel green offer a wide spectrum from delicate peppermint and aqua to the yellowy colour of a Golden Delicious apple. Like yellows, pastel greens sit well with neutrals; a tonal combination of creams and buffs with greens from chartreuse to duck egg can feel as calm and serene as you could wish. Pale wood is the perfect material for flooring and furniture in this instance. As with most Pastels, this scheme needs clear daylight to bring out the range of tones. Minty greens are a traditional bathroom choice but this is by no means the limit of their scope. Used as a colour-wash, shades of

opposite Shades of lilac coupled with sheeny fabrics, make this bedroom a stylish and serene haven.
left Black vinyl flooring is a successful choice here, giving an edge to the surrounding tones of lilac.

above Pastel greens, with their fresh, outdoor associations, are amongst the most relaxing colour choices you can make. As with all pastels, they are at their best in natural daylight.

aqua can be mixed with neutrals and white to form the foundation for a restful, beach-inspired space like a conservatory or even a bedroom. They can bring freshness and a lively look to a kitchen or playroom, especially with a splash of a balancing colour such as red from the opposite end of the spectrum.

Surrounding style

Pastels make a wonderful canvas on which to introduce existing items of furniture and well-loved bits and pieces. You might find you are able to retain your carpet, as long as it isn't patterned with orange dots or brown swirls. If it does have to go, take a look at the boards underneath: perhaps

they could be painted or limewashed to match the softness of the walls. Alternatively you could make a really strong statement by having, say, black floors and pastel walls. Surprisingly, the black will not appear to dominate. Instead it will punctuate a pale room and give it definition.

Woodwork should be cream rather than white, because the northern light responds much better to slightly muddy shades than pure ones. Brilliant white is a very distinctive colour which can leave surrounding shades looking rather dirty, while Naturals will create another subtle layer of visual interest without disrupting the harmony of a room. As far as furniture is concerned anything is acceptable, from distressed pieces to ultramodern ones. Pastels can be a great deal more flexible than other colour families, so while wood, metal, stone and glass all suit their calming environment, a brave, eclectic mix of

old and new, like a carved Indian table topped with a highly modern ceramic bowl, can also work well.

Finishing touches

Curtains can be floaty and pretty, and because pattern is a plus in a Pastel colour scheme they are an ideal way to introduce it. Similarly, you can add lots of accessories such as cushions and throws, because they will all work well together. You can also use bold pieces like heavy picture frames, chunky candlesticks and oversized pots with this sort of colour base. The problem can be knowing when to stop, because you could end up with a very chintzy room, with too many bits and pieces to have real impact.

above and above left The versatility of the Pastels is reflected in the variety of accessories with which they can be used, from heavy geometric forms and rustic materials to intricately fashioned, more contrived pieces.

Vivid vision

Vivid colours are by no means universally loved. The boldness of Moroccan blue, Chinese yellow, Grecian pink and Irish green is utterly uncompromising and so is not to everyone's taste. These colours are brimming with passion and vibrancy and will shout for attention as you walk through the door. You may love them or hate them, but you certainly cannot ignore them. Vivids radiate emotion and energy, bringing out the best in extrovert, confident types who like to wake up in the morning fired with enthusiasm for the new day.

Do you dare?

They are certainly not new, but they will require courage if you are used to living in a more muted environment. They demand that you live up to them and enjoy their boldness, and are incredibly rewarding when done well. There is no point even considering this family of colours for your home if your wardrobe contains only black and oatmeal, but if you have some fiery red, gutsy orange or punchy purple, you might well love a Vivid colour scheme. From a design point of view Vivids are fantastic to use because you can completely change the character of a space with nothing but a pot of paint. Having said that, these paints are not the cheapest. The brightest colours are often the most expensive because they contain so much more pigment than other shades. However, their impact makes them worth every penny.

Using vivids

To live happily with the Vivids you have to start by really wanting colour of this intensity. Then you need to find the ones you really love (see Know yourself, page 13). The Vivid palette is about solid wall colour that gives a

below Vivid colour combinations can create quite dazzling results and are certainly not for the faint-hearted. Be certain that this is what you want before you commit yourself!

above Metallic finishes enhance the glamour and excitement of the Vivid colours and, coupled with low-level lighting, will create an exotic mood.

room an instant facelift. It is not about a single red sofa or green cupboard. The power of this palette comes from being surrounded by colour in every direction. As the walls reflect colour they take on even more vibrancy. Vivid rooms need plenty of light, particularly natural light, to prevent them feeling austere by day. For night-time choose halogen lighting as it creates a crisp, clean effect, and install a dimmer switch for control. Candlelight can also be very effective in strongly coloured rooms. A dramatically decorated dining room, lit by candles, can take on another mood-enhancing dimension.

Colourful past

You might think that Vivids are only suitable for large rooms, but you would be wrong. A very small one can gain character through being painted in a really strong shade, perhaps midnight blue or even black. Period homes with wonderful features can take colour in large doses, but so can modern architecture. The interesting thing about this palette is that you can choose either the historic or the modern route. We often forget that the faded tones we see in old houses were once bright and intense. Reds, yellows and blacks were combined to sumptuous effect 200 years ago. Before that the Elizabethans, and even the ancient Egyptians, were familiar with dynamic colour.

Building blocks

Because the striking effect of the Vivid palette lies in solid, flat colour,

you do not need texture on the walls. In fact, you must prepare the surfaces meticulously to make them as smooth and unblemished as possible before paint is applied. It may seem as though you save time by skimping on preparation, but in the long term you'll spoil your efforts as the eye will focus on imperfections and miss some of the impact of the colour itself.

It requires skill to use Vivids well as they work best in rooms that are layered with colour. Walls are the starting point and the core of a Vivid scheme, but there should be a sense that everything else has followed on from them. The look is breezy and confident, so build up rather than tone down the furnishings to maximize the impact. Vivids also respond well to dramatic contrast; brilliant white and deepest black are two of the strongest, most dynamic foils for these colours. Rooms that make a striking statement with colour are apt to lose their edge if they are too cluttered, so you must be something of a purist to maintain the effect. Old newspapers, toys and shoes will ruin the serenity of any scheme. The approach is almost minimalist, but with the impact of several fantastic colours on top.

Heating up

Hot colours are probably the most exciting of the Vivids. Their instant, breathtaking impact makes them a joy and a thrill to work with. It goes without saying that sizzling shades are not for the timid, but if you are looking for ones that will set a scheme alight, then fuchsia pink, hot orange and sunbeam yellow will do so perfectly. They are so energetic that they create a real sense of excitement, either jostling for attention alongside each other or teamed separately with black. Interestingly, their intensity means they dominate black, which becomes a frame for these more powerful colours. Few others, with the exception of emerald green and brilliant turquoise blue, would have the power to achieve this. Set against pure white the hot colours can dazzle with freshness and crisp clarity, while touches of exotic gold will create a dramatic, more mysterious mood.

below The walls are just the starting point for a Vivid scheme, where layers of vibrant colour build up through furniture and accessories.

雲城花 誠意

above Red is so powerful that, even used in a restricted way, it can appear to be the dominant colour. Here its effect is tempered by a warm parchment shade on the walls and ceiling.

Regal red

Red is lively, vibrant and bold, one of the most outrageously extrovert colours of the Vivid palette. It is hardly surprising that many people are too terrified to use it in decorating. This is a pity, because few colours can cause

a stir in quite the same way as red. A little goes a very long way so you can create a wonderfully dramatic effect without actually touching the walls. Red is the ideal accessorizing shade, with flowers, rugs or picture frames being some of the most common ways of introducing it in a controlled way that is far removed from the overpowering impact of a red wall. Team red with black or grey for an architectural feel or with green and perhaps a touch of silver for a more muted approach. Do remember, though, red is such an uncompromising colour that, whatever you put with it, the overall impression will be of a scarlet room.

It is useful to be aware of the effect of red on a room. Firstly, it reduces light substantially so you need to have enough for this not to matter. Secondly, it gives the illusion of the walls and ceiling drawing in and the intensity of the colour can almost be intimidating. A clever way to overcome this is to reverse the traditional order, keeping the walls neutral and painting the woodwork red. Skirting boards, picture rails and window frames are often off-white to make them invisible in the room, but painting them red can be the means to achieving the full impact of the colour without sacrificing the sense of space. Pure white walls would be too jarring a contrast, but a creamy buttermilk shade is warm and substantial enough to balance the scarlet woodwork.

Red is so gutsy that accent colours must be chosen with care. Gold is a glorious companion as it emphasizes red's rich, exotic quality and works beautifully with cream. Gold wax can be rubbed on to scarlet gloss-painted woodwork to add texture and a subtle sheen. If you wish, you can avoid the overly sumptuous look this colour

combination could create by scaling down the use of red and gold in the room. Smaller amounts will maintain the interest but take away the force. It is also important to punctuate a rich cream, red and gold room with a darker, heavier note so that the look is not overwhelming. Navy blue has weight, giving the eye somewhere to pause. Chocolate brown is also a possibility, which is why dark wood

below Dark wood furniture works well with scarlet: brown comes from the same family as red and has the strength and weight to balance it.

works so much better than pale with these colours. It has the same tone and can therefore take the strength of the red.

Blues brothers

This side of the Vivid palette extends from ultramarine through bright peacock green to turquoise, emerald and lime. These are mostly cool shades that, despite their intensity, will open up rather than shrink a space. Their obvious aquatic associations mean they have traditionally been popular for bathrooms and kitchens and they can lend character to very small spaces although, like all Vivids, they benefit from good light. The current trend for using glass in interiors, seen in glass bricks and sandblasted items like shelves, table-tops and even hand basins, suits the green and turquoise end of this spectrum especially well. This family can also look stunning with all kinds of metallic finishes: think of brightest blue walls decorated with subtle, gleaming copper leaf or stainless-steel fittings in an aquamarine-painted kitchen. Black and white are useful companions to these shades: the fresh combination of electric blue and brilliant white is a classic with enduring appeal, while black brings a graphic quality to the green tones. Set acid lime-green against bright fuchsia, or cobalt blue against red, their opposites on the colour wheel, to create some real indoor fireworks.

above and above left With their strong, simple forms, geometric shapes are the natural partners of Vivid colours. **opposite** Raw materials like stone slabs allow the eye to be drawn first towards the patches of Vivid colour that decorate the walls.

White and bright

The Vivid colours suggest a room that vibrates in front of your eyes, yet they can be introduced in a way that still retains an overriding sense of calm. The basis of this idea is a brilliant white room, a crisp, clean canvas that creates a dynamic partner for bold splashes of colour. Percentages are the key to this scheme; it hinges on the amount of colour you choose to

anything more ornate, like trompe
l'oeil frames for example, would
destroy their effect. That aside, the
idea is a simple one that could easily
be transported into any home.

The new trend in applied
decoration is to create effects with
blocks of different colours instead of
using techniques like colour-washing,
stencilling and sponging. Rather than
painting one wall a slightly different
shade from the other three, you can
scale down the blocks and have lots
of them. Use your colours randomly:
a symmetrical pattern would be a
mistake as the eye would follow the
pattern rather than taking in the
colours. If you are not sure you have
the confidence to paint your walls in
this way, experiment first on scrap
paper with felt-pens or art paints.

Blocks of bright colour are perfect
for a small, dark or meanly
proportioned room because the
geometrical shapes can introduce
a sense of order. They also work well
in modern houses where there might
not be many architectural features
to draw the eye. Not only does the
pattern provide masses of visual
stimulation, it also gives the illusion
that the room is bigger and taller than
it actually is. This is partly due to the
way in which white creates an
impression of space around the
colours. Pure white has a totally
different character from cream or
magnolia. It demands attention,
whereas the warmer shades can
blend into the background and
become invisible. The power of white
makes it the ideal canvas for Vivid

introduce on to the wall space, floors
and furniture. In a room with white
walls you could add cubes, stripes
and circles in techno-rainbow shades
of brilliant green, pink, yellow, red and
blue. Imagine you are creating a piece
of modern art and the finished result
will certainly be fabulous. The beauty
is that it doesn't matter if you place
colours that scream and clash right
next to each other provided they only
cover a small part of the overall area
proportionally. The skill is in knowing
when to stop. Blocks, stripes and
circles are enough on their own and

colours. It is not so much a backdrop as a frame and in this respect performs a similar role to black. White will inject energy into a dark, low room, but do check the artificial lighting. If it is poor, it will make the white look dingy, but well-positioned spotlights will bring your space alive.

Surprisingly, natural colours have an important role to play in a room that uses a small but vigorous amount of Vivid colour. Floors, windows and furniture should remain quiet and harmonious if you want attention to remain focused on the patches of colour on the walls. Nothing else

below Black and fuchsia compete here for centre-stage, so cream rather than eye-catchingly brilliant white is the right choice of backdrop.

should distract the eye from the wall decoration or vie with it to be noticed. Black furniture could be used but would look very stark against white, and therefore intrusive, and dark furniture would set entirely the wrong tone next to the audacious Vivids. Materials like concrete, paving slabs and unpainted MDF create a sympathetic look that does not fight with the stronger colours around it. They also add an element of texture that is important in a room full of brilliant but flat colour.

The new black

It might seem strange to home in on black in a chapter about Vivid colours, but it will play an important part if you want to use the palette well in a variety of ways. People are often afraid to use it in decorating, fearing it might look too sombre and funereal. But it becomes enormously enjoyable when set against colours that fight back fiercely. You might not have the courage to use it so boldly, but don't ignore it completely. There is no better way to offset a really striking feature like a dazzling painted floor than by using black. Combined with pinks or yellows in geometric forms it will introduce a retro flavour. Admittedly, a little will go a long way and you would probably not want it at the heart of your decorating schemes, but it is well worth experimenting with it to introduce an occasional touch of hardness and edge.

Surrounding style

As far as floors are concerned, virtually anything will work with the Vivid palette. Natural floors, be they parquet, painted or sisal, look great and carpet in bold colours like midnight blue, red or black works well too, though these very rich shades can be expensive. Pale limed or bleached wooden floors would not be suitable as they lack the strength to work with Vivids. Any style of furniture can be used so long as it is bold enough to sit happily in a Vivid setting. Antique pieces in dark woods would look wonderful, as would modern designs in graphic black.

Finishing touches

A Vivid room is all about drama and theatre, so windows should echo this feeling. Coloured banners that create huge blocks of colour (see Painted banner, page 236) look sensational in a boldly coloured room, as do more traditional curtains made from masses of fabric tapestry or damask. However, a Vivid room is not the place for clashing pattern as there is enough going on already.

Nor would the prettiness of flowered swags be appropriate. You can opt for very traditional or very modern windows, but a smart, tailored look is the one to aim for. With high colour on the walls you need to carry the

effect through the rest of the room. If your sofa is beige, for example, you will need to pile it with huge cushions in punchy colours to bring it into the scheme. A simple wooden table will call out for an exotic-looking runner and plain curtains will relish the exuberance of a pompom edging. Reflective surfaces look stunning in dramatic settings, so mirrors are an absolute must. Also try experimenting with layers of metallic varnish over matt paint. Fabrics are very important. Throws, rugs, cushions and window treatments all combine to accentuate richness and character. Flowers are also integral to this scheme, the stronger and more dramatically coloured the better. With so many rich ingredients, the presence of light and shadow will add a further twist.

below left Mirrors can only add to the excitement of a Vivid scheme, allowing hints of bold colour to be reflected on to every part of a room. **below** The most intense colour combinations will not feel intimidating when incorporated into a design through small accessories, like cushions.

Deep delight

Of all the colour families, the Deeps have the most confidence. They do not give a hoot about fashion trends or design. They are classic, grown-up and show that you, not your home, are in charge. These are the earthy shades of an autumn garden: sage green, denim blue, terracotta, aubergine and ochre. They are typically English colours. They suit our northern light because they have a muddiness that is easy on the eye. Deeps are not muted. They still have force, but are not fierce. Reminiscent of hand-stitched tapestries or old-fashioned rose chintzes, Deeps are nostalgic without being mawkish, romantic but not sentimental. This family is comfortable, unassuming and incredibly easy to live with. It could not be further away from the Naturals in its philosophy. Here there is no sense of paring down possessions or focusing attention on to a single perfect object. Everything and anything goes in these interiors. An old rug, dog-eared books, a hand-knitted shawl and children's cardboard models can all blend comfortably. For those who aspire to a cosy life with family, pets and possessions accumulated over the years, this palette might be the right one.

below Structural features, such as the wooden beams, low ceilings and flagstone flooring, give this room an aged, comfortable atmosphere, making the Deeps an obvious choice

Using deeps

Like the Pastels, Deeps are easy to use because any shade goes with any other so long as you keep to the same tones. You can happily mix brick reds with linseed yellows, sage green with denim, or dusty pink with pigeon grey. This is far from being a modern look, but it has a character that suits a more timeless approach. The key word here is personality. These colours are a world away from fashion catwalks or the whims of design gurus and have little to do with the buzz of the moment in Paris, Milan or New York. Their success is linked to

Placed next to other Deeps, a warm orange, although just a few shades down from the zingy Vivids, takes on a more mellow character.

what you yourself can bring to a room: your treasures, the way you live, the imprint you make on your surroundings. They have everything to do with comfort, cosiness and character and create an enduring style that will still appeal when other current fads have waned. Deeps have a traditional flavour and something of a rural feel. Their roots are in the earth, contrasting with the modernity of the Pastels, the global outlook of the Naturals and the urban edginess of the Vivids.

Old English shades

Period houses blossom with colours like these, which bring out the charm of rickety sash windows, warped wooden doors and old brick floors. Deeps are exactly the sort of hues found in English country houses that have seen better days. The look of faded grandeur is one that has been exported throughout the world, particularly to the USA and Japan, and these colours are its foundation. English women have a worldwide reputation for interesting, individual and slightly eccentric style and the Deeps colours reflect this mood. They are not so sympathetic to modern spaces because they lack the definition needed by contemporary architecture. Stick to the idea of consistent tonal value and you can layer a huge number of colours and textures within a room so that it takes on the mellowed charm of a traditional country house. Deeps are a great choice if you hate decorating and want to do it as rarely as possible.

Rather than regularly starting afresh, this palette lets you just keep adding layers to your home.

Deep inspiration

Good light is a boon to all colour schemes but is not as essential to the Deeps as it is to some others: their muddiness means they can cope with the dullest of rooms. This makes them ideal for our changing seasons because their beauty is not lost in the greyness of winter. Nonetheless, you will enjoy them more if you light them well with table lamps and wall lights as well as from overhead. Be careful about the other colours you introduce. Deeps do not sit easily with Pastels, Naturals or Vivids. They need shades that match their tonal value. This means playing down accent colours which could unbalance the whole scheme. Instead you can introduce contrast through textures – a beautiful damask throw or velvet cushion that will lift the subtle colours around it. Pattern has a place but, like the accents, must not be allowed to dominate. The Deeps work best in an unstructured scheme, so avoid too much coordination. For example, a sofa with a matching footstool and curtains would be too regimented and tailored. The aim is to create the feeling that the scheme has gradually built up with the accumulation of various possessions.

Very berry

Although reds in the Deep family have certainly lost some of the fire seen in the Vivids, it has been replaced with a rich, glowing quality reminiscent of purply-black cherries, overripe cranberries and the papery skins of red onions. These are full-bodied but mellow, insouciant shades that can be layered almost infinitely one on top of another. Because they are so all-enveloping they are a wonderful choice for the ultimate comfortable living room, where you can pile a well-worn brown leather chair or sofa with a mixture of throws, blankets and cushions. Fabrics are vital to this look and cosy checks,

below Unlike other palettes, Deeps do not demand fabulous daylight and their gentle tones respond well to more subdued lighting.

chenilles and damasks combined with floor rugs and tapestries will bring a sense of a style that has evolved over time. A flavour of the exotic can also work, with kilims and Eastern-inspired fabrics on the floor and walls, and terracotta pots and baskets evoking the feel of personal treasures gathered from travels.

Ochre, denim blue and forest or sage green make gentle accent colours, and textures such as velvet and linen will add further levels of interest. The palest you should venture is a warm buff or parchment shade if a neutral is needed but, as with all the Deep colours, to step outside the tonal value of the reds could produce a jarring effect. These restful heavy shades do not demand too much light. They really come into their own on winter evenings when candles or firelight will be all that is needed. Alternatively, uplighters and lamps will provide enough glow to maintain a warm, subdued mood.

Sage advice

Soft sage green is a relaxed, easy colour to live with because it has no sharpness and will not take your breath away. It contains lots of red, which takes out any acidity, yet is still fresh, clean and confident, ideal for injecting new life into a tired space. It combines well with other shades of the same tone and is classic enough to look good for years. This makes it a good choice for a kitchen, where frequent decorating would be very

opposite The rich cream and restful green of this kitchen show a light aspect of the Deep colours.
below and below left Sage green works well as either a solid or a colourwashed finish, making it a useful tool in blending new items with existing fittings, such as doors.

disruptive. Sage green will lend itself well to either solid colour or paint effects like dragging or sponging and this means it is ideal in a room that contains both new items and pieces salvaged from a junk shop or market. The old furniture will probably need layers of flat colour to disguise its original state, whereas the new timber may look all the better for having some grain showing.

If you want to follow the fashion for using blocks of colour to draw attention to the intensity of a shade, rather than breaking it up with a paint technique, a heavy, warm cream makes the perfect foil for this shade

of green, where brilliant white would be too harsh and intrusive. In a kitchen the blocking idea can be reinterpreted to divide the room into upper and lower halves. The base units can be painted in sage to anchor them to the floor while wall units in a lighter shade will prevent the overall effect being too heavy. A boundary line, perhaps of tiles in a darker green, will give more definition.

Lemon yellow is an excellent accent colour in a sage and cream room as it has a touch of sharpness that can lift the other tones. Tomato red would also work very effectively or, for a little more drama, black could be introduced. Naturals, such as unpainted brickwork or earthy floor tiles, match these key shades well without distracting attention from the main story. They will act as a foil for the more definite colours but prevent the whole scheme from becoming too overwhelming.

Glowing embers

Bold colours like mustard and burnt orange are more often associated with children's rooms than adults' and are only a couple of notches down from the sizzling hot Vivids, yet they can be used to great effect in both settings. For the kids there should be

below Mustard yellow, burnt orange, scarlet and blue make an exhilarating combination for kids' rooms, showing the versatility of the Deep colours.

alone can produce drama and a buzz the moment the door is opened. They would also be a good choice for a lively, bustling family kitchen. Scarlet is an obvious but still striking accent shade and, for something a little more subdued and unusual, try silver in keeping with the current strong trend towards metallics.

Sweet as honey

Rich, warm and inviting, a honey-coloured scheme will bring character to any room, making the shade one of the most versatile colours of the Deep palette. It is also one of the most satisfying to work with because it floods a room with colour without being aggressive. Because it is so dense, it can seem to shrink a space and is therefore best used in a fairly generous area with good light – although it doesn't insist on the natural sort. It reacts well to artificial light, creating a seductive atmosphere that is wonderful for evening rooms.

Shades of honey are just the starting point for a surprising range of possibilities. The addition of another strong colour like chocolate brown lends guts to a mid-tone that could otherwise appear too cloying. Brown is a natural companion, and the earthy combination evokes a sense of Africa that could inspire a naïve-art look with block printing and hand-painted lines. Alternatively, it is possible to achieve quite a different result by combining ochre with jewel-like greens, blues and metallic gold for a rich palatial feeling – or with soothing creams and

above An action-packed scheme like this one shows just how versatile the Deeps palette can be.
opposite Tones of honey, ochre and orange lead, quite naturally, to a modern take on colonial or African-inspired design.

plenty of colour and action on the walls so that there is interest and stimulation wherever they look. For grown-ups, opt perhaps for mustard as a wall colour and disperse burnt orange, punctuated with other Deeps like flax blue, through the room. Blue furniture can create a Provençal feel in a mustard or burnt-orange room. A touch of black will give an edge.

Colour influences mood and these shades are definitely stimulating. As such, they are absolutely ideal for a playroom or den where colour

whites for a honeyed softness. Black would create a strong, dramatic effect, perfect for a softly lit dining room.

Ochres and honeys demand a bold approach if they are not to submerge you. They can take heavy, chunky shapes, and prepossessing dark brown furniture therefore works much better than pale woods. Furniture legs are a way of breaking up forceful colour and leading the eye through to the wall beyond. Excitement or risk is essential to any successful scheme, so break the rules and add a shade that demands attention. Tangy orange brings zing and a hint of sharpness that punctuates and grounds the yellow.

Acid green or cherry red would make a similarly-powerful statement, but orange works particularly well because it comes from the same family of earthy tones as honey and brown.

Surrounding style

Plain wooden floorboards topped with faded rugs work best with the Deep colours. Natural alternatives like sisal and coir can look good but are best as a base for carpets and rugs. Traditional hard floors like tiles, brick or stone make the perfect backdrop for the other earthy shades in this palette. However, a fitted carpet is likely to look too smart and it would

below Dark, hand-painted stripes and distinctive furniture-legs help break up solidity, easing the impact of this rich honey shade.

be difficult to find a suitable colour. Dark wood is the ideal for furniture as glass and metal would look very out of place in a Deep room. Scour junk shops and markets for old pieces that can be spruced up just a little, remembering that the more distressed and aged they look the more at home they will seem. Not everything has to be the height of good taste, and the philosophy behind the Deep palette is that you should do what feels comfortable for you.

Finishing touches

Windows can either be treated very simply or very elaborately. Fabric, rather than blinds or shutters, really comes into its own with the Deeps. Generous swags and tails would be appropriate as long as they are not too new or smart-looking, and simple curtains hung from a wooden pole would fit in equally well. Old-fashioned chintzes with full-blown roses are perfect, so seek them out at jumble sales or soak new ones in tea for a faded, aged look. Accessories are very important to this look and you will need plenty. Heap sofas and chairs with big tapestry and velvet cushions, cover shelves with photograph frames, pot plants and bowls of pot-pourri, and walls with homely paintings. The result can be a smart 'shabby chic' effect or something more Bohemian, with the flavour of an artist's studio-cum-living room, where children's playdough and cardboard works of art sit happily alongside more conventional family treasures.

above left A Deep scheme should be anything but co-ordinated, creating the impression of a naturally accumulating and ever-evolving scene.

above Simple accessories like woven grass mats and a hand-made papier-mâché bowl emphasize the relaxed, all-embracing nature of Deep colours.

Manage that makeover

TV makeovers can appear a touch unreal – a lacklustre room is transformed with the wave of a wand. Yet we know it's hard work and forethought that get the job done. Give yourself time, the right tools and the guidance of *Changing Rooms* designers, and that wand can be in your hand.

Transformation tactics

There is undeniably a great deal to think about when planning a room makeover. Colour, lighting, storage and style all have their part to play and must be thought about in relation to one another. Deal with each in isolation and you run the risk of having a confusion of looks rather than a cohesive structure. Costings must also be worked through in detail. Time invested in thinking, making lists and looking for inspiration is time well spent.

Cash concerns

A strictly limited budget is all part of the fun and drama of a television makeover, but it is also a very real and important consideration in your own plans. Once you have a figure in mind it is sensible to stick firmly to it, even though you may have to compromise on some aspects of your design. If you really cannot bear to change your ideas, the alternative is to halt the plans until you have saved up the extra. It also makes sense to give yourself a reasonable financial safety net in case you uncover any serious problems such as damp or faulty wiring which cannot be ignored. It will be a bonus if you don't need it, but if you do, you'll be very glad it's there.

Fixed features and functions

Of course you will be limited by the sort of space you have, including not only the size of the room but its shape, light and any structural features, but once it's cleared take the opportunity to study it with a fresh eye. Be guided by what is there, rather than trying to impose a whim on a totally unsuitable

opposite Angular rooms can be softened by introducing circles and curves.
below A little ingenuity can make something appealing from the least promising feature.

location. It has been the trend over recent years to preserve, or even put back, period features like fireplaces, picture rails and ceiling roses but this really is a matter of personal taste. Not all these features are appealing, so keep a critical eye in assessing what should stay and what should go.

Similarly, you must consider the function of the room. For example, you can run wild visually in a child's one, but you also have to think about the durability of floors and furniture and the wipeability of surfaces. Again, think of this as a source of inspiration rather than a hindrance. Function should always underpin design and there are a few rules of ergonomics that are designed to help our lives become more efficient. For example, just how much space is required around a dining chair, and what is the critical distance between sink, fridge and cooker in a smoothly operating kitchen? It is very easy to get carried away by beautiful bedlinen or heart-

below Function and style meet here: the perfect position for every item in this Japanese-inspired room has been carefully thought through.

stopping paint colours, but these are of no consequence if you do not make the space work well for you.

Design direction

The best way to clarify your ideas and gain an impression of how they are working together is to build up a sample board around your selected colours (see pages 10–65 for information on planning your scheme). If you plan to change soft furnishings, ask for fabric swatches. Use bigger pieces for areas like curtains that require large amounts of fabric, and smaller ones for accent pieces like cushions or rugs. If the curtains are going to be full, with swathes of fabric, bunch up your swatch to give the same impression. Remember that light affects colour so always view paint and fabric samples in the room itself, under the lighting conditions that will be used.

Paints and fabrics are the obvious items to use when putting together a sample board, but don't be afraid to use colours and textures from objects such as a piece of china or a collection of photographs, which may evoke a certain feeling or trigger an idea for a theme. Natural elements too can inspire. Try placing pieces of granite, stone or wood next to paint and fabric to see how the colours and textures work together. Remember, this is the time to experiment. It costs nothing to dabble on your board with combinations you might have only dreamed about, but the next stage is to buy the paints and fabrics for real and mistakes can be expensive.

Designers in action

Here's how Linda Barker arrived at the scheme for her Restful living room (see page 86). Her initial inspiration came from pictures of crumbling fresco artworks. As she looked through holiday photographs and books on Italian architecture,

above Absolutely anything that inspires, be it seeds, twigs, ceramics or string, has a place on a working sample board.

references for paint effects and decoration began to come together. One of the strongest ideas was an ornate wall scheme coupling a classically inspired acanthus-leaf motif with bold calligraphy and setting this against a palette of earthy pigments and plaster pink. The calligraphy was inspired by engraved lettering on the foundation stones of an ancient Roman villa. Linda incorporated natural elements such as twigs and leaves and used a variety of different greens, from bright acid to mellow pistachio, for fabrics and accessories to balance the gentler colours of the walls and fireplace.

Paint facts

Colour is probably the first aspect you will consider when planning your design. For instant and inexpensive transformations paint is unbeatable, but it isn't just a straightforward matter of slapping your favourite colour on to the walls and hoping to forget about whatever might be underneath. Walls and woodwork may require preparation first and there are different types of paint for different surfaces, a range of finishes and various ways to apply them.

Surface preparation can often take longer than the actual decorating, but doing it well will ensure a durable, clean finish so cutting corners at this point is not advisable. For a really smooth result on walls you need to paint directly on to plaster so you'll have to remove wallpaper or woodchip. The quickest way to do this is to hire a steam stripper (see Mexican

above Paint is a fast and satisfying way to bring about an instant transformation and its potential extends far beyond plain wall colour.

kitchen, page 92). A light sanding will 'key' a plaster, painted or varnished surface ready for painting. Sugar soap is perfect for washing down painted woodwork prior to repainting.

Paints fall into two categories: water based and oil based. Water-based paints have several advantages. They are kinder to the environment, don't smell so strongly and are easier to use as brushes can be cleaned in water. With advances in paint technology, they are now virtually as tough and hard-wearing as oil-based finishes.

Water-based paints Emulsion is the most commonly used paint for interiors. It is easy to apply, dries quicky, usually within an hour, and, as mentioned above, brushes are easily cleaned with water. Special one-coat emulsions are now available. Cheaper products will have poorer covering power. Once dry, the surface is wipe-clean but not washable. Emulsion paints are available in flat finish (matt emulsion) or mid-sheen (vinyl silk or satin emulsion). Mid-sheen products can withstand more cleaning than matt finishes. Water-based gloss for woodwork is a recent development.

Oil-based paints These paints are slower drying than water-based ones but they are tough and washable. Brushes must be cleaned with white spirit solvent, which is also

Clean brushes that have been used for water-based paints in warm, soapy water. Rub the bristles right up to the heel of the brush with your fingertips and rinse until the water runs clear. Hang the brushes up to dry by the hole in the handle, so that water runs away from the metal part and air can circulate around the bristles. Clean brushes with white spirit after using oil-based paint. Squeeze the bristles with a rubber-gloved hand and rinse again in white spirit.

Roll it out

A roller will cover a wall with paint with amazing speed, but there is a technique to using one successfully. Use a short-pile roller on smooth surfaces and one with a longer pile for a rougher, textured area. Don't overload your roller as paint will spray everywhere. To avoid this, fill a sloping ribbed paint-tray about one-third full, dip the roller in and roll it over the ribs to distribute the paint evenly. If you have to stop work for a short while put the roller in a plastic bag to prevent the paint drying out. A synthetic sleeve will give the best finish with water-based paint, and can be easily cleaned with warm, soapy water. Choose a lambswool one when using oil-based paint. Buy the best roller you can afford, as a cheap one will roll unevenly and smear the paint.

used to dilute the paints if necessary. They are available in matt, mid-sheen and gloss finishes. The mid-sheen, known as eggshell, satinwood or semi-gloss, is suitable for walls and woodwork. It is washable and easy to apply. Gloss has a very shiny finish and is generally used only on woodwork. Matt, or flat finish, although oil-based, looks like an emulsion. It is regarded as a specialist paint, and is only available in certain outlets.

Primers Primers are used to prepare surfaces for painting and are available as either oil- or water-based products. Oil-based ones are suitable for stone, concrete, wood, chipboard, hardboard and plywood. Acrylic primer is water soluble and is used on soft- and hardwood, MDF, chipboard and plywood.

Brushing up

There are many types of brushes on the market, made from natural products like bristle, and from synthetic fibres. Ordinary, flat-bristled decorator's brushes are ideal for woodwork and plaster. For 'cutting in' (the name given to defining the outline of the area you are going to paint, such as along the line where a wall meets the ceiling) and painting awkward areas use a smaller brush, anything from 1cm (¼in) to 5cm (2in). Flatter wall surfaces require 7.5cm (3in) to 10–12cm, (4–5in) brushes. Stencilling brushes, designed for stippling paint through a stencil, have short, stiff bristles cut flat at the ends. Artist's brushes are available in a wide variety of shapes and sizes and are the right tools for fine hand-painting.

below Mirrors are a key decorative accessory, adding drama by reflecting colour and light around the room.
bottom Keep your eyes open for that one-off junk shop bargain that will finish a scheme to perfection.

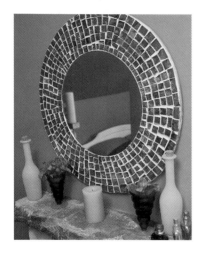

Colour crisis

It is not uncommon to put your chosen paint on to the walls and then get cold feet. Don't panic if it doesn't look right – a tiny paint sample will never be able to give you a true picture of the effect of a colour on four walls. Also, any colour can look off-putting without flooring, furniture and accessories. You cannot really tell whether you like a colour or not until you have added all the other ingredients to the room. If it looks right on your sample board, try to have the courage of your convictions and stick with it. Everyone gets it wrong from time to time so if you really feel you have made a mistake, don't despair. Look for a way of making the colour less solid by using a paint technique or applied decoration. This might be some kind of mural (see Sun mural, page 150), a horizontal stripe (see Painted wall stripes, page 126) or bold stencilling (see Stencilled blind, page 172).

A contemporary solution would be to paint just one wall in a startling shade and the other three in a more sombre colour. If you feel your chosen colour is looking too cold and stark, you can add a slightly warmer shade containing lots of magenta. Pour the two colours into a tray and keep mixing until you have the effect you want. Be sure to keep a note of the proportions of each shade so that you can make up enough paint to cover your area.

New from old

To keep within your budget it makes excellent economic sense to make the most of what you already have. When you want to revamp everything, it is likely your hard-earned money will already be spent before it comes to furniture. However, old or dated items can be given a new guise with paint and other treatments (see the dresser in Mexican Kitchen, page 92). Old picture frames can be painted or even gilded for a totally fresh look that won't cost the earth. Junk furniture, too, can offer surprising results and the best bargains often turn up at car boot sales, where you can haggle over the price. Check out markets and charity shops. Skips can be another source of one-off gems, particularly if a house is undergoing conversion, but do be sure to ask the owners first and check carefully for woodworm. Salvage yards are also a boon as they

can yield all manner of furniture and eccentricities. (Check the Yellow Pages under architectural antiques or salvage and reclamation.) Flooring can set you back a long way financially, so don't assume you know what's beneath that old carpet – you might be pleasantly surprised by original tiles, or well-preserved floorboards shouting for paint. Even curtains and blinds can be successfully rejuvenated with a little effort (see Linda's restful living room, page 86, and Graham's turquoise bedroom, page 110).

Shapes and sizes

Using pattern can be a bit intimidating and the choice of what is 'in' or 'out' is very personal. The secret of making it work for you is to break the rules. So many patterns become associated with one particular setting – tartan in a baronial-style home, toile de Jouy in the bedroom and sprigs in a country cottage. You can have enormous fun mixing patterns in unexpected ways provided you stir in plenty of plains to avoid a jarring confusion. As with colour, you can

learn to use pattern to play visual tricks. Like bright colours, large eye-catching patterns can draw attention away from one area and on to another. Bold ones can make a room seem bigger and busy ones can introduce a textural quality. Take care with symmetrical patterns as they will show up the flaws in a less than perfectly proportioned room. If you are nervous about using pattern, the simplest, most foolproof approach is to take one motif and repeat it throughout the room in different scales and using different materials. This makes a strong statement that will not confuse the eye.

It is also a good idea to have one object that dominates your scheme in terms of scale and creates a focal

above left Although daunting, used with conviction, pattern can add personality and atmosphere to a room
above Modern pieces can mix happily with old flooring and furniture: a flexible approach will give your home a relaxed, uncontrived air.

point. This could be anything from a really bold stencil on the wall to an oversized bedhead. Large-scale ideas work especially well in small rooms because they trick the eye into thinking the space is larger than it really is. For example, floor to ceiling curtains will make a low room seem higher, and a wide stripe running horizontally around a space will make it appear broader.

Touchy stuff

Texture has largely ousted pattern as the most important design ingredient after colour, although both add another layer of interest in a room. Surface interest visually alters tones as different textures reflect light individually. Fashion designers have demonstrated how it is possible to create the subtlest colour variations with different weaves and finishes in fabrics, and tempting materials like suede, chenille, fake fur and velvet are all now well established in the home. A room makeover no longer means just adding new colours, it also includes layering textures to give definition and interest. It is often the texture that makes a key piece so special, whether this is some rosy crushed-velvet curtains or a smooth stainless-steel worktop. Textures, like colours, work together to produce excitement and energy in a room, through contrast. A shiny piece of furniture like a glass table needs the hard edge of perhaps a rough stone bowl to offset it. If all the textures are

above and above left Texture demands as much attention as colour. It affects the way we perceive the subtleties of tone in fabrics and hard surfaces alike.

too similar, the overall effect is bland and uninteresting, the same as if only one colour were used. (See Natural order, page 18, for more information on using texture.)

Make light of it

Lighting is one of the most important ingredients of decorating and is now generallly recognized as being fundamental to the success of a design. Without it textures are flattened and even the most beautiful room will look dull and unimaginative.

If you think about your home carefully, you may realize that the reason you seldom use a particular room is because the light makes it stark or uninviting. Poor lighting can be depressing while good lighting is uplifting and energizing. In this sense it is as influential on our moods as colour and contributes enormously to the quality of life.

Natural light can be one of the best features of a room. Observe your space to learn when the sunshine is at its best, whether this tallies with the times the room is used and how the light moves around. Try leaving doors open to see if it spills in from an adjacent space. Think about whether you want to keep the light or block it out, and how it affects your decorative scheme (see Design direction, page 71).

Artificial lighting has two functions: firstly, to take over when natural light fades, and secondly, to boost light when needed. Think initially in terms of function. Is there sufficient light to

read, cook or shave? Then look at the ambience created. Is the light sympathetic to the space and does it evoke the atmosphere you want? Each room in your home will require different combinations of lighting.

Living room Flexibility is the key here, as you will need a combination of generally diffused lighting and local directional lighting for specific tasks

below and below left Artificial lighting should be beautiful as well as functional. Provided they fulfil your needs, choose lights like accessories, to enhance the overall look.

like reading or sewing. Accent lights may also be required to highlight a particular area or display.

Bedroom Downlighters are best for gentle overall light, with table lamps for a softer atmosphere. Bedside reading lights must be tall enough to throw light on to the page and task lighting for applying contact lenses or make-up will also be necessary.

Bathroom Safety regulations are strict wherever water and electricity are both present, so dimmer switches must be fitted outside a bathroom. All electrical fittings should be enclosed to avoid water penetration and possible shorting. Downlighters or wall-mounted fittings can give good light, but avoid unflattering fluorescent strips. Spots fitted around a mirror are perfect for shaving or making-up.

Dining room Atmosphere is all here so use a combination of lighting, including candles with strategically placed mirrors. You want a subtle, flattering light that still allows people to see what is on their plates.

Kitchen Task lighting is essential for everything from chopping vegetables to handling hot pans safely. Spotlights on tracks are perfect and undercabinet lights are ideal for illuminating work surfaces.

Porches, stairs and hallways Porches and stairs must be well lit for security and safety.

below and below right Effective storage is essential for a harmonious home. Cupboards and shelves are just one option and many modern solutions are decorative as well as useful.

Lamps or uplighters fitted with low-voltage bulbs will ensure that hallways are sympathetically lit and that visitors are greeted with a warm glow. You might want dimmers for low-level night lighting on landings.

Home office Task lighting is critical here. Lighting must focus directly on the page or computer screen without causing too much glare. Book shelves and storage areas also require appropriate lighting, perhaps lamps or spotlights.

Space to store

Storage is an essential consideration when you plan your design. Clutter is unattractive and frustrating to live with, so you need to think about dealing with it as part of the overall scheme. Storage is also integral to function: cupboards, shelves, alcoves, drawers, rails and boxes are the means by which a room can be made to work well on a practical as well as an aesthetic level. A room makeover gives you the ideal opportunity to sort through and organize your possessions in a logical manner. Anything that is not used on a day-to-day basis should be packed up and put away so that items essential to daily life are easily located. Donate the rest – unwanted gifts and dubious sale buys – to your local charity shop.

Collections such as ornaments can be incorporated in your room, displayed on walls, shelves or table-tops, and glass bottles and containers work well in a bathroom. Trivial objects displayed together can gain importance and really start to

above and left Whether pictures or pottery, a group of objects will take on a presence and have more impact than single items.

pull a scheme together. Shelving is essential for easy access to books, while cupboards are the answer for things you want to have to hand but not on display, such as a video recorder. High street shops are bulging with baskets, boxes and other gorgeous storage ideas, and you may find yourself encouraged to be more orderly if you have some attractive dedicated places in which to put things.

Anna's circle living room

Unless your home happens to be in an unusual building, it can be difficult to make it stand out from the crowd. So many of us live in predictably shaped rooms with neutral colour schemes, all adding up to a humdrum interior. Anna Ryder Richardson was called in to energize the living room of a 1940s-built home on a former RAF base. The room was totally functional, with good daylight and no obvious drawbacks, but it felt long and narrow and had no personality. The focal point was an unappealing gas-fire with a brown-tiled hearth. There was a bland beige carpet and the walls were painted a dull cream. Double doors led to the adjoining dining room but, as they were kept closed, they gave the appearance of a firmly shut cupboard dominating the wall opposite the fireplace. The only hint of colour was in the pale-blue sofa and chairs.

Style scheme

Anna could see that the room had the potential to make people gasp as they walked in. Her main objective was to disguise the uninspiring angles by introducing some dominant curving forms that would break up the straight lines and add softness, texture and movement. The idea of circles as a theme seemed perfect, as it would lend itself to both large- and small-scale ideas. The pale-blue furniture and neutral carpet limited the colour options, but rather than fight this, she incorporated them into an airy scheme of blues and creams, adding a contemporary space-age touch with silver highlights.

right and above Curves and circles, both horizontal and vertical, introduced a sense of energy and movement to this featureless living room while fresh blues and whites with touches of silver kept a feeling of lightness.

Walls and doors

In a room with good light, like this one, the choice of colours is really not restricted. Anna was aiming for a blue and cream look, to match the existing furniture, and her plan was to break up the two long wall spaces as much as possible. A massive fire-surround achieved this on one side. On the other side, the wall was painted a paler blue, and contrasting blue vertical stripes of different widths and shades were added at one side of the dining-room doors. This added interest, emphasized height and deflected attention away from the length of the wall. The two shorter walls were painted a fresh, pale cream to keep the room light and airy. Using masking tape is the simple way to keep painted stripes straight but, particularly on an uneven surface like wood-chip, it is important to make sure the edges of the tape are firmly stuck down so that paint does not seep underneath.

The flat dining-room doors were still the outstanding feature in this part of the room, creating a dense, dead-looking block. The solution was to take them off and cut a big upright half-moon shape out of each one, making a symmetrical pair. The holes could be lined with either flexi-MDF or stripped-down battening and a groove was cut down the centre of each, using a router. Then semicircles of clear acrylic, cut out with a jigsaw, were slotted into the grooves to make twin windows that allowed a view straight through to the dining room beyond. This instantly broke up the solid doors; giving a hint of the space outside and making the whole room seem wider and more open.

Fireplace

Although it was to be non-functional and purely decorative, the fireplace was to remain the focus of the room, and Anna's vision could not have been further from the original installation. A really large-scale, dominant feature like this can make an entire room feel more spacious and draw attention away from a low ceiling or narrow width.

The first task was to remove the old gas fire. Never attempt to do this kind of work yourself. It really is a job for a qualified gas engineer, so always call in a CORGI-registered

below Some chunky pebbles from a garden centre were painted with the remains of the wall colours, and then coated with a layer of matt varnish to make a simple decorative detail in the centre of the fire surround.

professional. Once the old appliance had been disposed of safely, part of the fireplace was chiselled out with a lump hammer (always wear protective goggles for this) to make an aperture into which the new structure would slot. This was a huge MDF construction, made in four sections, spanning almost the entire length of the wall and reaching up virtually to the picture rail. It comprised a symmetrical pair of segment-shaped structures complete with neat cupboards, which filled the alcoves either side of the fireplace. Two further separate pieces were screwed flush to the chimneybreast and a tube of flexi-MDF, built onto the lower one, gave the look of a grate. The four pieces fitted together to form a semicircle and the surface was grooved with a router to form a subtle grid pattern. Painted off-white, the surround created a stark contrast against the rich blue wall behind, instantly attracting attention. The old-fashioned tiled hearth was also chiselled out using a lump hammer and the remaining shallow hole levelled with cement to match the rest of the floor. It was replaced with a smooth, white-painted semicircle cut from 18mm MDF using a router on a trammel bar, a type of compass-arm. As it was simply ornamental, the hearth could just rest on the floor.

Furniture

Unless it is your pride and joy, it is very easy to allow a TV to dominate a living room as they are usually

large, black objects, perched in prominent places. A TV cabinet is the answer if you would rather not look at the set when it is switched off, and Anna came up with a design that blended perfectly with the curves and circles in the room. Built from MDF, it was a wedge-shaped cabinet that fitted conveniently into a corner, and had a pair of sliding doors in its rounded front. Following the overall theme, the door handles were simply cut-out circles. The basic structure consisted of two quarter-circles of MDF, attached to solid sides, with flexi-MDF forming the curved front panels. Frosted polypropelene doors could slide along grooves cut into the front

above A wedge-shaped TV cabinet made economical use of a corner and the top doubled as a display area.

above and right The curvy theme and metallic highlights were carried through in every detail, including wall-lights, discs of mirror and rounded vases decorated with silver leaf.

CHECKLIST

DAY ONE

Have gas fire removed
Paint walls
Chip out aperture for fireplace
Remove hearth
Build and install fire surround and new hearth
Cut and insert contrasting carpet
Cut panels out of doors and fit acrylic panels

DAY TWO

Build and paint tables
Build and paint TV cabinet
Make and paint new hearth
Paint fire surround
Fit curtain poles and hang curtains and blind
Make and hang acrylic chandelier
Spray rubber rings
Fix up mirrors and shelves
Make cushions

edges of the top and bottom. When open they were hidden behind the curved MDF panels.

Like many others, this room had a matching pair of sofas. Instead of the predictable arrangement of placing a single coffee table between them, two chunky, round tables, one slightly larger than the other, were made from flexi-MDF, topped and tailed with discs of MDF. They were painted pale blue and the tops decorated with a scattering of round steel washers held in place by circular sheets of transparent acrylic, about 5cms wider than the table tops.

Flooring

For a living room or bedroom, carpet is the ultimate choice for comfort and warmth underfoot. As it is an expensive form of flooring, it makes sense to opt for a neutral colour that will suit the room even when you redecorate. Colourful rugs are a quick way of adding some interest, but Anna came up with another idea for giving an inexpensive lift to an unexciting carpet. Remnants and off-cuts are often substantially cheaper than standard lengths and she tracked down a left-over piece of pale grey-blue carpet that would fit in with her scheme. A semicircle, mirroring the fire surround, was marked out on the existing carpet, using a compass made from string with a nail at one end and a piece of chalk at the other. Then the shape was cut out of the existing carpet using a craft-knife. The string compass could then be used again, to cut an identical piece from the new carpet. This fitted perfectly into the gap and the edges could then be joined and sealed with carpet-joining tape. This has to be stuck onto the underside of the join and then melted with a hot iron to create a strong bond. The eye-catching swathe of pale blue broke up the uninteresting expanse of floor and reinforced the circle motif in the room.

Accessories

Accessories are the simplest and most inexpensive way to inject interest and personality, and build up a theme. Here, the colour scheme and circle motif were further strengthened through Anna's choices. A glass gold-fish bowl of painted pebbles filled the round fireplace. Cylindrical and curved vases and bowls in blues, whites and silvers were dotted on budget pre-cut 6mm toughened glass shelves. Anna created a modern take on a chandelier with circles of opaque acrylic. These were cut out from off-cuts, using a drill bit hole cutter and their edges smoothed with fine sandpaper. The discs could then be either sanded all over, or sprayed with glass-etch spray to create the frosted effect. They were then joined in strings by inconspicuous fishing-twine and

suspended around the existing light fitting. Discs of 4mm mirror formed a column on one wall, increasing the sense of light and space.

Finishing touches

A dash of humour adds a touch of originality to any room, and here Anna used her circle theme, incorporating inflatable rubber rings, which were sprayed silver and simply stacked on the floor making a fun, tactile and visual point. Comfy cushions in shades of blue and cream were made on a sewing machine and piled on the sofas, and a simple white blind covered the window, diffusing the light.

above and below The circle shape proved to be very versatile, adapting to both large and small-scale designs and working in a variety of materials.

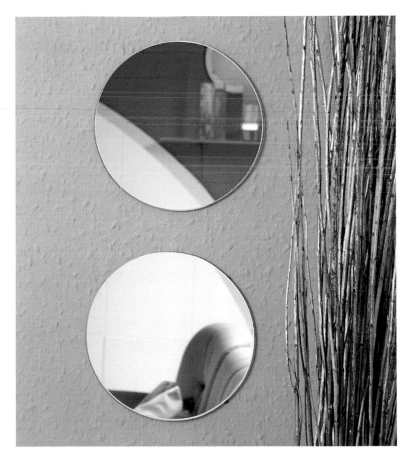

Linda's restful living room

Many of us live in Victorian properties and so know the pros and cons of this particular type of building. Charged with bringing a fresh look to the living room of a flat in a Victorian terraced house, Linda Barker quickly pinpointed the typical period features that could be turned to her advantage.

On the plus side, there was a beautiful, original wooden floor in good condition and large double French windows that opened out on to the garden, giving the room a bright, airy feel and good daylight. There were also spectacular high ceilings with the potential for putting something dramatic overhead to show them off. The layout of the furniture made the most of the central feature, a fireplace with original mouldings, but this was flanked by an ugly metal stack-system housing the TV and hi-fi. The fireplace had been painted in jarring colours and, along with a sofa and chaise longue, was in need of some restoration. The limited time and a budget of just £500 called for a truly creative approach.

Wall finish

A generously proportioned room such as this one has the space to show a detailed wall treatment like the one Linda planned as the anchor of her design. It involved three processes: the découpaged leaf decoration, the fresco paint effect and finally the calligraphy, and took up much of the time on the first day.

The découpaged leaves were the first task. Photocopies of the acanthus-leaf design were cut out and glued with border adhesive (a special glue for sticking wallpaper on to wallpaper) at dado height around

above A simple paint technique was applied to the border of découpage leaf motifs to produce an aged effect.
right Linda's transformation restored elegance and style to this beautiful room.

Prime and wax fireplace

Wash walls and woodwork

Paint two base colours on to walls

Apply photocopies to walls

Wash over third paint colour

Add top coat of paint, plus finishing glaze.

Screw electric connector blocks to branch, remove centre light and hang chandelier (consult electrician)

Move chest and drill logs

Finish waxing fireplace

Begin and complete calligraphy

Rehang photographs

Make side lamps from twigs and copper wire

Decorate screens to hide TV and hi-fi

Dye muslin drapes

Move TV unit

Paint curtain poles, reverse curtains and sew new headings into place

Re-cover chaise longue

Make calico throw and cushions

Hang antique Venetian mirror over fireplace.

the room. When dry, they were wiped over with a dilute mixture of emulsion paint and water (1:4 paint to water) and a damp cloth, building up areas of colour. Finally, a layer of equal parts of white emulsion and scumble glaze sealed the découpage and the result was a dramatic border with a hand-painted look. The fresco effect was achieved by layering two emulsion colours, using a 10cm (4in) brush. The paint was applied patchily and the colours were blended while still wet to build up an interesting textured

above The wonderful patterns, made by the calligraphy on the fresco walls, formed an attractive focal point that added to the formal feel of the room.

surface. Finally an inspiring piece of poetry was transferred on to the fresco surface, using an overhead projector to throw the image of the script on the wall. The letters were traced in diluted acrylic paint, using a fine, stiff-bristle paintbrush, and the design was topped with a coat of

clear acrylic varnish for protection. The overhead-projector technique was also used to decorate a pretty, three-panelled screen for masking the unsightly TV and hi-fi.

Fireplace and accessories

Victorian living rooms are generally dominated by a fireplace. These are often quite grand, sometimes made of marble, or with intricate mouldings or tiles, and as such are almost impossible to ignore. Today, with central heating making the function of a fireplace obselete, drawing attention to the structure and details with a simple finish and stylish accessories will ensure that it never looks out of place, whatever the décor.

Here the fireplace had beautiful detailing, just crying out to be highlighted, and Linda decided to repaint it in white acrylic primer, then wax it to bring out the delicate designs of the moulding. The entire surface was lightly sanded and then painted with a coat of the primer, ensuring that this covered every tiny indentation. An antiqued look was achieved very simply by rubbing a dark-coloured furniture wax over the fireplace with a pad of wire wool. Rubbing harder on the raised parts of the moulding allowed the wax to build up more heavily in the recesses, giving a highly authentic result.

When you are revamping a room, whether it's a simple rethink of the layout, or a complete transformation, don't forget about items from other parts of your home which could be brought in to give a different look. An array of glass containers from the kitchen, in tones of lemon and lime, sat perfectly on the mantelpiece of the living room, creating a striking contrast against the warmer muted fresco colour of the walls. The heavy wooden mirror above the fireplace was exchanged for an elegant Venetian one discovered in the bedroom. To one side of the fireplace Linda created a miniature gallery, which perfectly matched the overall scheme, using four family

photographs. Four sheets of handwritten script were photocopied and the copies cut to exactly the same dimensions as the existing framing mounts, then painted with a weak solution of cold tea for an aged effect. Using spray-mount, the photographs were stuck to the scripts, which were secured to the mounts with sticky pads. The frames were then replaced.

Sculptural twisted willow twigs arranged in a green glass vase echoed the graphic quality of the calligraphy on the walls, and small touches like a branch of fresh mimosa and a bowl of crisp green apples added to the scheme.

below and bottom Repainted and waxed for an antique look, the handsome fireplace now merited its focal position. Although it could not be lit, candles added an inviting glow.

Lighting

Lighting is an important yet often overlooked tool which plays a major part in creating interest and the kind of inviting atmosphere Linda had in mind for this room. The central chandelier was made from a large branch picked up in the local park and suspended from the ceiling in place of the original light fitting. Five separate lighting cables were secured through the branch by an electrician. Bunches of feathery twigs, gathered from the garden and bound around the bases of the existing floor lamps with copper wire, transformed the lamps into stylish pieces which created soft, interesting pools of light in the corners of the room. The plain shades were trimmed with dried pressed leaves attached with a drop of PVA glue, and then bound with a decorative strand of natural-coloured raffia. Rustic-looking candlesticks, simply fashioned from lengths of silver-birch logs with small holes drilled into the tops, held candles for highlighting the plaster-effect surface inside the fireplace. (When handling any electrical appliances, be sure to observe safety precautions at all times and never allow twigs to come into contact with a naked bulb.)

Furniture and soft furnishings

Curtains and upholstery can be very expensive, so before you sink your hard-earned savings into fabrics do consider whether you can reuse what you already have. Plain fabrics like muslin or sheeting can easily be dyed in your washing machine for very little outlay, and the range of dye shades available now is very comprehensive. You may also think about altering existing curtains, perhaps adding a contrasting fabric to ring the changes.

As Linda's budget would not stretch to new curtains she came up with an ingenious way of recycling the existing ones. They were taken down and the header tapes were stripped off. The raw edge of each was turned over on to the reverse side to meet the lining and both edges were then concealed under a band of hessian tape. A new coat of paint refreshed the curtain poles before the curtains were reattached

below Crisp greens and lemons, in the form of some decorative glassware brought a touch of acidity, contrasting effectively with the warmth of the wall treatment.

on the reverse side by simple ties sewn on to the hessian tape. The buff-coloured linings of the curtains linked in perfectly with the natural tones in the room. To add more drama, and for contrast, floaty muslin sheers were dyed a deep green in the washing machine. Chunky knots were tied in the ends and the sheers were hung at the window on old curtain wires.

With a heavy chest of drawers and unattractive metal shelving either side of the fireplace the room felt unbalanced, so Linda advised that the layout of the furniture should be rethought. This is a quick, no-cost way to freshen up any tired-feeling room. The television and hi-fi were resited and screened and the chest was moved to the wall opposite the fireplace, allowing this decorative element to take pride of place as the focal point of the room. Two key pieces of furniture, the sofa and chaise longue, were both in need of new covers, but the constraints of the budget would only run to a simple throw for disguising the old sofa. Linda chose a light creamy calico and added a few coordinating cushions made up on a sewing machine, bringing softness into the room. For the chaise longue she selected a fresh pistachio green, different from the other shades in the room. Avoiding an exact match prevents the overall effect appearing contrived.

The process of transforming the worn-looking chaise longue into a striking item of furniture was quick, and called for minimal stitching. The

fabric was stretched over the seat base and roughly trimmed to fit around the back rest. With the chaise longue turned on its side, the fabric was stapled to the frame, keeping it as taut as possible and working from the centre of each side outwards. The corners were folded neatly underneath with a series of small tucks before the excess fabric was trimmed away. The backrest and side armrest were re-covered in the same way, tucking any excess fabric into

above Food can sometimes be the ultimate accessory. This carefully placed bowl of green apples was the perfect finishing touch to the room.

the sides. The finishing touches were to hand-stitch a shaped piece of fabric over the stapled edges on the front of the curved arm section, and to re-cover the bolster, adding a large self-covered button to secure and hide the gathered ends.

Linda's Mexican kitchen

A fabulous kitchen is top of many wish lists and you may long to rip everything out and start from scratch, but your problems are often simply down to poor planning. A fresh look at the layout will help clarify where the trouble spots are.

Assuming your existing units and appliances are basically sound, they can be reorganized and given a fresh face. As Linda Barker demonstrated in her vibrant Mexican-inspired makeover, it needn't cost a fortune to achieve something close to the kitchen of your dreams.

In this bland, all-white kitchen interrupted work areas were the biggest headache, and a yawning space under the worktops, where a base unit could have fitted, was attracting more clutter by the day. The room was also on two levels with a small step down to a dining area at one end. Linda sensibly decided to create two clearly defined zones at the other end, one for cooking and one for preparing food, rearranging the wall units so that ingredients were to hand in the preparation area.

Worktops

Once the dishwasher had been resited and replumbed and the room cleared, a new worktop was installed over the dishwasher. This was to form the basis of the food-preparation zone, with wall units transferred from the opposite side of the room. The worktop section was measured, cut to size and propped on the dishwasher carcass and a new side made from MDF. It was secured to the back of the wall with a metal bracket and rough edges were neatened off with a chrome joining strip.

above and right A little reorganization, plus a swap from clinical white to sizzling shades of chilli and indigo, helped alter this kitchen almost beyond recognition.

Walls and floor

The walls had been decorated with a vinyl-type covering and this had to be removed before painting. Paint applied directly on to plaster will give the cleanest finish and a hired steam stripper is the least gruelling way to strip walls. Follow the manufacturer's instructions, and score the surface of the wallpaper with the edge of a screwdriver or craft knife to allow steam to penetrate the paper. This will make the process quicker and easier.

Here, the stripped walls were sanded with a hired hand-held sander and a pale emulsion base coat was applied with a roller, ready for a colour wash. When this was dry a spicy terracotta emulsion (Flambeau) was mixed one to one with water and then roughly painted on with a 10cm (4in) brush. The brush marks gave the walls a washed, mellow finish.

Vinyl flooring is a practical choice for a kitchen and is available in a great range of colours. If you are covering a small space, you may even be able to pick up an offcut large enough to do the job very inexpensively. Linda replaced the old lino with a bargain offcut of solid blue vinyl that fitted perfectly with her terracotta and blue scheme. The amount required was worked out by multiplying the widest width of the floor in metres by the longest length in metres. The brass treads around the step area were unscrewed and the lino was pulled up. If it had been impossible to remove this, it could have been left in place and the new flooring could have been installed on top. The lino was used as a template for the vinyl. An alternative would have been to lay sheets of newspaper over the area and join them with masking tape to form the correct shape. The subfloor was thoroughly cleaned with a kitchen-floor cleaner and strips of double-sided carpet tape were laid across the area. The vinyl was then laid over the top and pressed down by hand, starting at a corner – starting from a straight edge is an alternative. Treads were replaced as necessary and excess vinyl was fitted neatly under the kickboards.

Window treatment

The windows in a kitchen need some kind of dressing, especially if you plan to eat there in the evenings and want to create a soft, welcoming atmosphere with low lighting or candles. Blinds are convenient as they don't take up space

below A budget offcut of dark blue lino provided a practical, inexpensive flooring that fitted in perfectly with the overall colour scheme.

unnecessarily or attract grease and dust as readily as curtains might. Linda added a splash of pattern in the kitchen area with a simple Roman blind in a heavy Indian cotton check. She measured the length and width of the window and cut the fabric to size, adding 5cm (2in) all around for turnings. (Extra fabric would be required if the blind were to hang outside, rather than inside, a recessed window.) To create the characteristic crisp folds, three separate rod pockets were made to hold dowelling across the back of the blind. Each pocket was made from a 7.5cm (3in) wide strip, cut to the width of the blind plus 5cm (2in) for turnings. The longest raw edges were pressed underneath using the smallest possible turning, and folded together. Then one of the shorter sides was turned under and pressed and the pocket was sewn around the remaining three sides. The drop of the blind was divided into eight equal parts and the three pockets were pinned across the width on the wrong

above The windows were dressed with checked blinds that picked up the terracotta shades, making a cheerful backdrop to the cosy dining area.

CHECKLIST

DAY ONE

Have dishwasher plumbed in
Move fridge-freezer
Fix new top over dishwasher
Strip wallpaper and prepare walls
Paint walls terracotta
Remove flooring and lay new vinyl
Remove and reposition wall units
Assemble fronts for cupboard doors
Saw MDF for unit doors
Start to prime, paint and wax doors
Cut and punch two tin panels
Paint shelving unit and dresser

DAY TWO

Complete cupboard doors
Make up and decorate bench seat
Sew Roman blind
Fix wooden battens and hang blinds
Cut table-top, secure legs, apply
paint and varnish

side of the blind: one three-eighths of the way down, one five-eighths down and the third at the seven-eighths point, so that the flap at the bottom of the blind measured the final eighth. The rod pockets were then stitched to the back of the blind, keeping close to the raw edges.

A batten was attached to the wall above the window to hold the blind in place (See Magic shelves, page 193) and two eyelets were then screwed into its base 7.5cm (3in) in from either end. Next, one part of a Velcro fastener was firmly sewn along the top of the blind and the other part of the fastener was stapled along the batten. Blind rings were hand-

sewn at either end of the rod pockets (a centre ring would also be needed for a longer blind) and 9mm (⅜in) dowelling rods were inserted. Lengths of blind cord were then tied to the lowest rings, threaded up through the others and then passed through the eyelets in the batten and over to the side of the blind. Finally, the two sides of the fastener were pressed together to hold the blind up and the cords were secured on a cleat at the side.

Cupboard doors

The cost of new kitchen units is generally prohibitive but this makeover illustrates the staggering

above The kitchen units were given a new lease of life with Linda's punched tin panels and simple paint treatment.

transformation that can be made with some innovative thinking. Linda decorated the existing cupboard doors with panels of Mexican-style punched tin (see page 210) plus a rich blue paint finish. The doors were taken off the units, their handles were removed and a base coat of matt emulsion (Pencil Blue) was applied. After an hour, when the paint was dry, a pad of medium-grade wire wool was used to wipe the surfaces over with a liquid wax (Dark Oak) to create an antique finish. The handles were replaced and the doors were reattached to the cupboards.

Furniture

Existing items often have the potential to be incorporated in a new look without too much effort. Linda easily revamped a basic pine shelving unit with a paint treatment. The shelves were sanded and then quickly washed over with a dilute terracotta emulsion, in the same way as the walls. When dry they were sprayed with varnish to seal and protect them. The pine dresser was given a new location and a fabulous new look with the painting and waxing technique that was used for the cupboard doors. The same beautiful blue was used to colour-wash a simple wooden chest. This was transformed into a storage bench with the addition of shaped MDF sides and a curved back with a typically Mexican lizard cut-out created with a jigsaw.

A budget table for the dining area was made from a sheet of 1.9cm (¾in) MDF and four shop-bought table legs. The edges of the MDF were sanded and short woodscrews were used to fasten the legs about 10cm (4in) in from each corner. The table-top was primed and allowed to dry for about an hour and was then decorated with a freehand Mexican-inspired design, using small match-pots of coloured emulsion. The paint was dry in an hour, and the design was sealed with two coats of spray varnish, allowing half an hour between coats.

Finishing touches

A hanging rack from the hallway was moved to the kitchen to hold utensils and big bunches of herbs above the cooker. Coloured ceramics, vases, urns and a candelabra were all displayed on shelves and surfaces, along with characteristic small tin vessels, all of which brought the Mexican theme to life.

below Well chosen details such as colourful ceramics, tin kitchenware, generous bunches of fresh herbs and a typically Mexican lizard motif all added to the impact of the design.

Graham's beige living room

 In a family home, the living room has to work hard, keeping the kids happy during the day, while providing a more sophisticated haven for adults after work. With dual demands it is all too tempting to opt out of the style stakes entirely and settle for a practical but bland look that will neither excite nor offend anyone. Graham Wynne was determined to prove that functional need not mean boring and that one living room can meet the whole family's requirements.

This rectangular room had a typically Victorian square bay window, with pink curtains hanging down to the window ledge, lending a dated feel. The bay was cluttered with furniture, including a chest in which toys were stored. The original Victorian fireplace had a cast-iron insert, but the patterned tiles and pine surround jarred with the rest of the décor. A burnt-orange sofa and armchairs dominated the dull cream walls and green carpet, and the immediate impression was uninviting. The room needed clarity, unity and a hefty injection of warmth.

Floor and walls

If you opt for bare, sanded floorboards, be prepared to find a less-than-pristine surface below your carpet. Boards may be rotten or damaged, especially in an older property, or you may have to remove old glue, tiles, paint or other remnants from a previous occupant's DIY attempts. (See Graham's turquoise bedroom, page 110 for tips on sanding floorboards). In this instance, old vinyl tiles, stuck down with bitumen, proved time-consuming and difficult to remove, but eventually yielded to persistence. This is really the only way to achieve a smooth, consistent finish

above and right The rough texture of the concrete fireplace was reflected in the accessories used in the room, such as these attractive tea-light holders.

DAY ONE

- Lift carpet and sand floorboards
- Remove fire surround and cover decorative tiles
- Build, paint and fit new fire surround
- Replace central ceiling lightfitting (consult electrician)
- Paint walls
- Construct and paint wall-hung storage boxes
- Construct frame for artwork and string with washing-line.
- Make and paint window seat

DAY TWO

- Spray-paint artwork
- Cut and refurbish coffee table
- Hang old unit doors as shelves
- Hang storage boxes
- Cover and attach foam cushion for window seat
- Hang blinds and add leather tabs and steel rods
- Make sofa and chair cushions

to your floor, so if you lack the strength, determination or time, choose an alternative surface that will conceal the problem.

The quickest and cheapest way to introduce energy and life to a room is with painted colour. Yellows make a wonderful choice in most locations in the home, as they are cheerful, welcoming and uplifting and will warm the chilliest spaces. Graham felt that three subtly different yellows, plus a khaki shade, one colour on each wall, would introduce the zest that was lacking, and also give a clean, modern twist to plain painted surfaces.

Fireplace

An original feature like a Victorian fireplace is not always an advantage and can detract from a more contemporary scheme (see pages 69–71 Fixed features and functions). If you feel reluctant to tear out a fixture completely, you can almost certainly disguise it without a great deal of difficulty. Fortunately here, the wooden surround was just screwed on to the wall and could be easily taken off and stored. It was replaced with a plain, box-style surround, about 20cm (8in) wide all around and about 15cm (6in) deep. This was built from fire-resistant MDF and grooved diagonally with a router at each corner to look like a three-sided picture-frame. The surround was painted using the same khaki shade as the wall, but with some sand mixed into the paint; the result was a coarse, concrete-like surface. Sheets of galvanized steel, cut to size, fitted

over and hid the patterned tiles, creating a smooth, shiny foil for the roughness of the surround. The result was a modern fireplace, achieved by disguising but not damaging an unsuitable original feature.

Storage

Space that is being used to its optimum potential should combine good looks, originality and practicality to satisfy both youngsters and adults; so living room storage often requires some thought. Secure places off the floor and away from the play area are necessary for delicate items such as the TV, hi-fi, and ornaments, and where space is limited, the walls can be efficiently used. Graham decided on a selection of simple, painted MDF boxes of varying shapes and sizes. Box shapes were built from MDF panels (varying between approximately 30 and 60 cms (1 x 2 ft) in height and width) joined with glue and screws. These were fixed into the alcoves using 5 x 2cm, (2 x 1in) battens either side of the fireplace. Graham chose a random arrangement, providing texture and visual interest in the room, as well as performing a valuable function. The clean-cut, geometric look worked well with the simple fire-surround, building the contemporary, angular look Graham was aiming for.

Toys can be the bane of many a parent's life. They have to be spread all over the floor to be enjoyed, but once the kids are in bed, no-one likes to be surrounded by lumps of lurid-coloured plastic or the entire cast of the latest children's show. A big toychest that can be filled each night is a good solution, but can take up a lot of room, so Graham hit on the idea of disguising a capacious toy-box as a comfy window-seat, with a lift-up lid. This was built very simply from MDF in the same way as the wall-boxes, but a hinged lid was added. The box was made to fit exactly into the bay window. The seat itself was made from a rectangular piece of foam, cut to size and covered with tan fake-suede fabric, bringing another textural element to the room and a contrast to the hardness of other surfaces. The seat was fixed to the lid with special spray-on foam adhesive, (foam mount spray). Finally the box was given a burnished metallic look with a coat of aluminium paint, which was applied with a stippling brush.

Furniture

The constraints of a budget often prohibit a new suite of furniture for a living room, so the existing one may have to adapt to fit into a new scheme. With loose covers, one option is to dye them. This is easy to do with a fabric dye in the washing machine, and will give an instant new look for minimal outlay, although, for it to work successfully, you must choose a shade that's darker than the original. Although a little more expensive, throws are another quick and simple way to revamp old soft furnishings. In this living room, Graham discovered pristine cream-coloured covers, ideal for his design, under the burnt-orange ones. However, with the practicalities of light-coloured furniture and young children in mind, he added some washable throws in pale shades over the top.

Graham's coffee-table transformation proves that even the

above and left Functional, but attractive storage space was a key requirement here. The box shelving provided ample space to store fragile objects and also displayed them to maximum advantage.

textured paint, (Make It Stone from Krylon). Finally, the centre of the glass top was masked off and the outer ring sprayed with glass-etch spray, leaving a clear circle, through which the crossed rods could be seen.

Items of furniture often become out-of-date long before they actually wear out. It can seem wasteful to throw pieces away just because you no longer like them, but, as Graham demonstrated, sometimes, with a creative approach, they can be partially recycled to produce something totally different. Here, an old, glass-fronted cabinet was destined for the skip, but Graham recognized the potential of the timber-framed doors, which could be converted into a pair of glass shelves, one hung directly below the other, to display ornaments. The slim glass panels were perfect for his clean, no-fuss look.

Shelves were created, firstly by fixing the doors horizontally to the wall on a pair of 5 x 2cm (2 x 1in) battens, one about 43cm (18in) above the other. High-tensile wire (available from ironmongers, DIY stores or yacht chandlers) was used to give the shelves rigid support at the front. To do this, two wall bolts with screw-eyes at the ends were fixed into the wall, about 43cm (18in) above the top shelf and in line with either end. Wire was threaded and looped through each eye and passed diagonally down from the wall and through holes drilled in the corners of the shelves. A fastening nut screwed directly onto the wire, and tightened above and below the shelf ensured

above The removal of the lower tier of the coffee table helped make it a worthy focal point of the room, while the addition of candles brought out the reflective qualities of the glass top.

most unappealing pieces may still have some life left. Subtle alterations to the shape and surface changed a dull, dated item into a stylishly modern centrepiece. The lower tier of this circular wooden table was cut out and replaced with a pair of crossed steel rods, visible both from the sides and through the glass top. Taking inspiration from the rough surface of the new fire surround, the table was then sprayed with a stone-coloured that it did not move. The wires then ran straight down, were threaded through and attached to the corners of the lower shelf in the same way, before running diagonally back to the wall where they passed through a second pair of wall bolts. The lower screw-eyes could then be tightened to take up any slack and ensure that the shelves were held securely.

Window treatment

A square bay window brings extra light into a room, which is a real bonus point, but the bay shape can be awkward to dress. Floor-length curtains can take up a lot of space and prohibit any furniture being placed in the bay, while sill-length ones can look messy. For a contemporary feel, plain blinds are the best choice and can look extremely stylish. Graham used four here, two for the long front of the bay and two for the two smaller sides. To lift the look, he cut small, neat squares along the bottom edge of the blinds with a craft knife, and threaded them with loops of budget-priced dark-brown leatherette using an eyelet kit. Chrome poles could then be threaded through the loops to add weight and make a neat finish.

Accessories

Sometimes a room needs one striking decorative feature that acts as a unifying element for the scheme. Graham drew on aspects of his design, such as the steel details and clean lines, and brought them together in an eye-catching wall-display that reinforced the theme of the room.

A simple 5 x 2cm, (2 x 1in) wooden frame was made, and holes, just large enough for a length of plastic-coated washing-line to be threaded through, were drilled at regular intervals all around the edge. Then, the washing-line was passed through the holes and was stretched across the length and width of the frame, keeping it as taut as possible, to create a geometric web pattern. A flat frame, about 10cm, (4in) wide was then cut out of MDF, and the wooden frame mounted onto it at a slight angle. This gave strength and hid any untidy knots. The washing-line and surround were sprayed silver, to resemble steel wires, (using Plastikote silver spray paint) and the frame hung with the flat side of the MDF facing into the room.

Lightweight breeze blocks painted beige served as candle-holders on the mantelpiece, echoing the concrete look of the fireplace, as did tiny stone-look tea-light holders on the coffee table. A cream rug softened the pale, bare floorboards.

Finishing touches

Simple vases and bowls and plump cream cushions added comfort and softness to the room, while glossy greenery in the grate, exquisite ivory lilies and some ethnic African pieces brought the serene room to life.

below A washing line was sprayed silver and used to make this spectacular geometric artwork.

Laurence's Arts and Crafts dining room

Natural light will have a major influence on the atmosphere of any room in your home, affecting when and how you use it. Before you decide on a decorating scheme you really need to take it into account, considering its strength and tone at various times of the day. It was the grey light in the dining room of this early Victorian house which immediately struck Laurence Llewelyn-Bowen. The owners had really struggled with decorating it, choosing a sunny yellow for their last painting spree. However, once their cheerful colour was out of the paint pot and on the walls, it became rather sludgy and dirty looking. Laurence advised that the room was north-facing and so had a cooler, bluer light than one with a southern aspect which would be filled with warmer light. In addition, the room would be mainly used in the evening with artificial light, so yellow was really never going to be a successful choice.

Style scheme

In this situation a return to the flavour of the original Victorian scheme would address the problem, rather than searching for a contemporary, but contrived, solution. Blues and greens might well have been used in a north-facing room like this one so, inspired by William Morris, one of the most important figures of the Arts and Crafts movement, Laurence decided to go for a shade of paint called Fern Green on the walls, complemented by a combination of two fabrics: a simple budget burgundy and a rather more expensive Morris print.

above and right Inspired by the Victorian designer William Morris, Laurence created a warm and welcoming dining room with green walls, printed fabrics and a stencilled freeze.

area, the site of the original hearth, in front of the chimney breast itself. The tiles simply required a thorough clean. This is quite easy to do using a mild solution of caustic soda (follow the manufacturer's instructions for this) and a hired floor-polisher. Afterwards, the floor was wiped down thoroughly with warm water and then buffed with plenty of liquid wax and soft cloths before being left to dry for an hour.

Walls, woodwork and ceiling

Painting is the fastest and most cost-effective way to bring an instant radical change to any room. Laurence went for a combination of solid Fern Green on the walls and a patchy effect for the ceiling, with a lively stencilled frieze to break up the plain areas. Matt emulsion in a cream shade called Chantilly was applied roughly with a brush to build up the mottled effect on the ceiling. The border between the ceiling and picture rail was also painted this shade, ready for the stencil design.

Laurence cut his own stencil, taking inspiration from the flowing leaf patterns in the William Morris fabric. He laid the design on oiled manilla card, beneath which a sheet of carbon paper was secured with the pigment side uppermost and used a pencil to trace around the outline of the design. When the design and carbon paper were lifted off the image was revealed on the undersurface of the card and he then used a craft knife to cut out the shape on a cutting mat. Stippling with

It's always worth looking objectively at existing features that can readily form part of a room transformation. A quick inspection beneath the carpet revealed an original black-and-red tiled floor, in keeping with the rich colours that would have previously decorated the house and a gift for Laurence's scheme. Much of the old furniture was used – a traditional pine dresser fitted in perfectly, together with a collection of gilt-edged plates. Once stripped of its varnish the dining table also sat beautifully with the style he had in mind. Laurence used chemical stripper

above Using existing pieces is part of the skill of a successful makeover. This pine dresser and collection of crockery fitted in perfectly with the new look.

and a scraper blade to take off the layers of varnish and washed the surface with warm soapy water. It was then protected with clear furniture wax, which was applied with a soft cloth and buffed to a sheen after half an hour.

Flooring

By a stroke of luck the Victorian tiled floor was still intact apart from a small

a dry stencil brush brought a spontaneous, flowing feel to the finished decoration.

The woodwork was painted with a 7.5cm (3in) brush and a single coat of ready-mixed emulsion in Fern Green, which was dry in an hour. The same shade was applied to the walls as a flat colour using a roller fitted with a short-pile emulsion sleeve. As the colour was so translucent, two coats were necessary, with an hour's drying time in between.

above and below The patterned frieze added to the overall effect, its cream background visually raised the height of the ceiling, bringing light into the room.

Fireplace

Opening up a concealed fireplace to create a decorative focal point in a room need not be a complicated task. Following through the Victorian theme, Laurence came up with a non-functioning fireplace that was characteristic of the period with tongue-and-groove boarding, ceramic tiles and shelf details. First the original grate was located by tapping with a small hammer on the centre of the chimney breast until a hollow sound was heard. Then the void was carefully exposed by tapping until the covering broke. The untidy edges were straightened up with sand and cement which were smoothed away with a trowel, and an architrave – a frame – made of bevelled wood with mitred corners, was fitted around the opening. First though, to determine the proportions of the architrave, the tiles were laid against the wall and a long spirit level was used to check that sides and angles were square. The architrave was secured to the wall with panel adhesive and supported with flat-headed nails hammered halfway into the wall while the adhesive set. To tile the space between the architrave and the opening, a layer of white ready-mixed

tiling adhesive was applied over the area with a notched spreader. The top left-hand tile was pressed squarely into a corner and then the next tile was added. The process was continued, with spacers being out between each tile, until the whole area had been covered. The tiles were left overnight for the adhesive to dry thoroughly before grouting.

Laurence's design included cladding the chimney breast in tongue-and-groove boarding. The way to approach this is to start at one side of the chimney breast, fitting the first board into the corner with the grooved edge against the wall. Apply panel adhesive, press in place and hold for 30 seconds. Tap long, flat-headed nails partially into the wall at the top, middle and bottom of the board to hold until the adhesive sets (about two hours), then pull them out with a claw hammer. Continue for the remaining boards, cutting the timber close to the architrave edge and skirting.

Shelves

Laurence suggested topping the the chimney breast and fireplace with a neat shelf at picture-rail height to give extra prominence to the focal area. Three 2.5 x 2.5cm (1 x 1in) lengths of pre-drilled timber were screwed around the three sides of the chimney breast, above the boarding. Using a paper template made in a curved shape with a right angle to fit against the wall at the top edge and a power saw, four corner brackets were cut from 5mm (¼in) MDF. Their positions were marked on the boarding, and the narrow edge of each bracket was pre-drilled. The brackets were then screwed to the wall with long, countersunk woodscrews. The holes were filled with all-purpose filler and sanded when hard (about 20 minutes). To finish off, three strips of MDF, 1cm (½in) deep and 20cm (8in) wide, were cut with a jigsaw, placed on the brackets and screwed into the timber lengths across the top of the boards to make the shelf.

The mantel shelf was made in a similar way, using the same bracket template and a slightly narrower MDF strip for the shelf. This time the fixing

below A throw of Morris-inspired printed fabric disguised an old chair and tied in with the patterned edging on the curtains. Having unearthed an original tiled floor, Laurence incorporated it into the design.

screws had to go through the shelf and into the narrow edge of the brackets themselves.

Window treatment

Curtains can be one of the most costly items to change, and even if you sew them yourself, the fabrics alone can eat into your budget, especially if you have a rich material in mind. As *Changing Rooms* designers are experts at controlling expenses, Laurence's spectacular slanting drapes didn't set him back nearly as much as you might imagine. The trick is to liven up lengths of inexpensive fabric with a strictly limited amount of a gorgeously extravagant one, and to hang the curtains in an eye-catching way that makes a statement. To create the diagonal shape, the drapes were strung with blind cords. Three 15cm (6in) strips of William Morris fabric were hemmed and then sewn around the three sides of each width of burgundy lining fabric. The length of each curtain was measured as the drop from curtain rail to floor, plus 5cm (2in) for turnings. A piece of iron-on buckram (pelmet stiffener) was covered with Morris fabric with the raw edges folded on to the wrong side. A length of 5 x 2.5cm (2 x 1in) battening attached above the curtain track formed a pelmet on to which the covered stiffener was fixed with Velcro. Each curtain was hung and then hand-gathered, starting at a point about one-third of the way up from the floor, on a diagonal line up towards the top inside corner,

allowing the folds to curve. The folds at the back of the curtain were caught with safety pins, which were pushed through both thicknesses of fabric at intervals of about 10cm (4in) along the diagonal. Blind rings were fastened to the pins and threaded with nylon cord, starting at the lowest point and working up towards the top inside corner. Then the cord was passed through an eyelet screwed into the pelmet batten, and passed down the outer edge of the curtain to be secured on a cleat. The workings were checked and the safety pins were removed, one by one, as the rings were stitched into position.

Accessories

Even though you may be aiming for a totally fresh look in a room don't assume you must replace absolutely everything, or that all your choices must be new items. Laurence revitalized old pictures, bringing them into his design simply by adding new frames and rearranging them in a bold, symmetrical pattern on the wall. He also hung some of his great-aunt's embroidery designs and unearthed an old forgotten clock in the loft, which tied in perfectly. Everyone's eye was automatically drawn to the tiled fireplace above which was displayed a beautifully detailed, mirrored overmantel that had been picked up for next to nothing in a local market. A simple throw made from a length of Morris-style fabric, complemented with plain cushions, completed the look.

above A symmetrical group of simply framed pictures made a strong statement against a plain wall and candles added an authentic Victorian touch.

Graham's turquoise bedroom

We like to think of bedrooms as sanctuaries, peaceful retreats from the rest of the world. Sadly, they are often nowhere near as calming as we would want. Graham Wynne's task was to bring some serenity to a dreary bedroom with pale walls, a green carpet and assorted furniture. Because it was a typical Edwardian room, there was great potential. Rooms from this period are usually generously proportioned, and here there was scope for a relaxing seating area. They also often have a fireplace and windows tend to be large so the rooms benefit from good daylight and can take bold, powerful colours. Graham felt strong tones would pull the separate elements of the bedroom together and, using the colour wheel principle of complementary colours, came up with a vibrant turquoise and fuchsia palette. Working to a budget always calls for an innovative approach as you cannot buy everything new. Graham transformed the roller blinds for next to nothing and revamped existing flooring and furniture, giving a totally fresh look to the whole room.

Flooring and walls

Sanding a floor is not difficult, but it is quite arduous and should always be your first task as an electric sander creates so much dust. Sandpapers are supplied with a hired sander, and the machine consists of two parts: a large sander and a smaller hand-held one. Make sure you read and follow the manufacturer's instructions for use.

For the bedroom, once the carpet had been taken away the floor was checked over carefully and any protruding nails or staples were removed with a claw hammer and

above Well-preserved floorboards offer plenty of options and are a boon for a budget makeover.
right Graham's design emphasized the best aspects of this room, its attractive dimensions and wonderful light.

7.5cm (3in) paintbrush, a solution of equal parts of water and white acrylic primer was painted on, brushing each board in the direction of the grain. When the boards were dry (at least 30 minutes) white primer was brushed over them, using the ends of the same brush, to leave a streaky effect. This took an hour to dry and was then sealed with two coats of satin varnish, allowing an hour's drying time between coats. As Graham had chosen a breathtaking shade of turquoise (M'Ladies Room) for the walls there was no need to embellish them with more than a coat of emulsion paint. This was applied to the main areas with a roller, and a small 2.5cm (1in) brush was used to 'cut in' around sockets and other features. The walls were left to dry for an hour.

Storage

A pair of wardrobes built into alcoves on either side of a fireplace is a fairly standard arrangement that, on the whole, provides a substantial amount of storage space in a bedroom. Although thoroughly practical, these wardrobes often lack a bit of style and the space on top of them is a magnet for mess. Here, Graham solved both these problems in one go by replacing each of the two pairs of doors – one larger set for the lower part and another smaller set for the top storage area – with a single taller pair that ran from the floor to the cornice, thus masking that top-of-the-wardrobe clutter zone. They are clad in attractive bleached-effect painted tongue-and-groove to tie in with the floor.

above Tongue-and-groove-clad MDF panels replaced dated wardrobe doors and the beauty of the fireplace was brought out with a quick touch of silver gilding wax.

pliers. Large nails were punched below the surface with a hammer and nail punch. Graham started with the large sander, fitted with coarse sandpaper, and worked it diagonally across the floorboards. The dust was brushed away and the floor was sanded again, this time in the direction of the boards and using medium-grade sandpaper. Then the smaller sander was used in the corners and to rub down the edges. The dust was again swept up and left to settle for an hour before being brushed up once more. Then, using a

The hinges of the wardrobes were unscrewed and the old doors removed, and the available space between the kickboard at the bottom and the cornice at the top was carefully measured. For each new pair of doors a 1.9cm (¾in) sheet of MDF was cut to these measurements with a jigsaw. A tape measure and pencil were used to mark the MDF down the centre and it was divided into two evenly sized doors with a jigsaw. Tongue-and-groove cladding was cut to the same lengths as the new door fronts and screwed on firmly, every 30cm (12in), by first drilling a pilot hole for the screw and then countersinking it. The holes were filled with all-purpose filler. Graham worked from the outside edge of the doors inwards to the point where the two doors met. The excess edge of the final piece of cladding on each door was then cut away using a jigsaw so that they came together neatly.

After 20 minutes' drying time, the doors were sanded down with medium-grade sandpaper, ready for painting. A 7.5cm (3in) brush was used to apply a coat of acrylic primer diluted with an equal quantity of water in the direction of the woodgrain. When dry, the doors were streaked in the same way as the floor and sealed and protected with a final coat of clear matt acrylic varnish, which dried in about an hour. The doors were then rehung with heavy gate-style hinges, allowing the longest part of each hinge to show on the front. Magnetic catches fixed on the inside with a

small screwdriver kept the doors closed and the look was completed with a gate-style latch to match the hinges. Finally, each wardrobe was given a neat finish with a section of white coving panel-pinned across the top of the wardrobe to meet the ceiling.

Furniture

Lacquered pine furniture has been popular for a long time, but Graham felt that the shiny finish of the bed and blanket box was looking a little tired and out of step with the fresh new look he was after. As the shapes and styles were still appealing, he suggested a simple, inexpensive update. The lacquered surfaces of the pieces were first lightly keyed with a medium-grade sandpaper block, then whitewashed in a dilute solution of acrylic primer and water, in the same way as the floor. The result was an interestingly patchy bleached effect. The furniture was sealed with a coat of clear matt acrylic varnish.

CHECKLIST

DAY ONE
Remove carpet and gripper rods
Sand, paint and varnish floor
Paint walls
Paint blanket box and bed
Construct new wardrobe doors
Dye rugs and stitch them together

DAY TWO
Paint and wax fireplace
Construct picture/display frames
Make table and tablecloth
Paint blinds and mirror
Trim and hang muslin drapes
Spray-paint wicker furniture

below The bleached effect achieved by a simple paint treatment gave the pine blanket box and bed an instant, inexpensive update.

A low table is the ideal piece to bring presence to a seating area, however small, and can be made and dressed without spending a fortune. To make Graham's table, a top was cut to size from MDF and four 5 x 5cm (2 x 2in) lengths were used for legs. With the legs kept flush to the table edge, the top was screwed on with long woodscrews. For extra stability, the sides were cross-braced with four lengths of 12 x 2.5cm (5 x 1in) timber screwed between the legs, again using long woodscrews. The white cotton calico for the tablecloth was cut to size by measuring from the floor up, across the width of the table and down to the floor again, and then from the floor up across the length of the table, adding 5cm (2in) seam allowance all the way around. The raw edges were turned under and stitched and the cloth was pressed. It was then thrown over the table and the corners were folded tidily underneath. A pair of cotton ties were hand-stitched and tied a third of the way down from the top of the table to hold the cloth neatly.

Window treatment

Although large windows flooding a room with light are wonderful, particularly if there is a spectacular view beyond them, they can be an expensive headache to dress. The bedroom already had nondescript, pale roller-blinds and Graham was able to incorporate these in a striking treatment that maximized the dramatic effect of the beautiful windows. The blinds were taken down and laid flat on a work surface. Pink fabric dye was diluted with about ten parts of water to one part dye and washed over them, a treatment that produces a pale pink when applied to white or cream blinds. After an hour's drying time, 5cm (2in) vertical lines were marked out on the blinds and masking tape was placed on these to form bold stripes. Then undiluted

left As the opposite colour to turquoise on the colour wheel, a small amount of fuchsia pink gave the whole room a sparkling, dynamic quality.

fabric dye was used to paint pink stripes around the tape. Brushing inwards from the tape prevented the colour seeping under it. After the dye had dried – a minimum of an hour – the tape was removed and the blinds rehung. The windows were finished off with ready-made white muslin drapes with ribbon ties sewn to the tops. These were hung from three straight metal curtain poles, forming the shape of the bay window.

Accessories

Bare floorboards often need something to make them feel a little cosier underfoot. Graham dyed three small rugs, using one box of dye (Deep Pink) for each, and stitched them together with bright turquoise thread. An old oval mirror was whitewashed and rehung vertically to give a more modern look over the fireplace. Detailing on the fire surround was highlighted with Treasure Silver gilding wax, applied with fingertips, and the mantlepiece was dressed with large candles. Honey-coloured rattan seating was sprayed with white car paint and piled with bright fuchsia cushions, floating candles and two table lamps added to the ambience.

above Blinds with broad bands of fuchsia pink made the generous bay window a focal point. With two distinct parts, the bed and the seating area, the room now felt more spacious.

Linda's multipurpose bedroom

Children's bedrooms can be a notorious 'no go' area, disorganized and full of clutter. If two or more are sharing, the problem is doubled or worse. Lack of space and storage options, plus a shortage of child-appeal, are almost always at the root of the trouble.

Linda Barker took up the challenge to transform a typical bedroom shared by two youngsters. The walls were covered in dated wallpaper and most of the floorspace was taken up by the two beds. Although clothes were stored in a chest outside the room there was nowhere much inside it for toys, and nothing in the décor to capture the children's imagination, let alone tempt them into keeping things tidy! Linda knew the look had to be colourful and exciting, while on a practical level storage and space issues had to be tackled. As the children were young, a themed design seemed appropriate and she opted for cheerful 'bottom of the garden' images and colours which she combined with Shaker-inspired peg rails, gingham checks and garden motifs for a really individual look.

Walls, ceiling and woodwork

Kids adore colour and are constantly on the lookout for new sources of interest and stimulation. Linda decided that fresh tones of bright, almost acid, green contrasted with bold blue would make a fabulous scheme for the room. In keeping with the folk-art feel she opted for a chequered painted pattern for the walls, inspired by the tones in a piece of traditional woven gingham.

To achieve an authentic gingham look, vinyl matt paint in three tonal

above and right Instant appeal is essential for children's rooms, so a strong colour scheme, like this acid green and bright blue combination was ideal.

DAY ONE

- Remove carpet and old curtains
- Staple down primed hardboard for floor
- Apply base coat and varnish to floor
- Paint walls and woodwork
- Mark up squares on wall
- Paint in gingham effect, and paint ceiling
- Make and install peg rail

DAY TWO

- Build and paint picket gates
- Apply paint and découpage to storage chest
- Stamp fabric for blind
- Make up blinds, banners and drawstring bags
- Fix up and decorate lighting collar
- Hang the Tarzan rope
- Paint chest of drawers
- Paint bed parts and assemble bunk beds
- Make flower and cockerel posts for beds.

shades of green – light (Chinois), medium (Lady Mantle) and dark (Sundew) – were needed. Fortunately the old wallpaper was not vinyl, so two coats of the medium tone were applied directly on top of it and also on the ceiling with a 10cm (4in) brush, allowing an hour's drying time in between. At this stage the woodwork was painted with satinwood paint of the same colour. This took two hours to dry. Linda then measured each wall carefully and began dividing them into 30 x 30cm (12 x 12in) squares. She drew horizontal lines across the walls with the help of a

spirit level, and used a chalked plumb line secured to the ceiling at 30cm (12in) intervals to mark the vertical lines. When the suspended plumb settled it was held tight against the wall and plucked, transferring a line of chalk on to the wall which was then traced over with a pencil. When the whole room was marked out the lighter and darker squares were painted in, using the piece of gingham as a guide to the right sequence of light, medium and dark squares. Each square was first outlined with a 2.5cm (1in) brush before being filled in with a 5cm (2in) one.

above Garden-style gates created a fun storage area that would attract the children's interest, hopefully encouraging them to put things away!

Flooring

Hardboard flooring is a practical and inexpensive option for smaller rooms like this, and has the added advantage that it can be painted any colour you like. Once the old carpet had been removed, new sheets of flooring-quality hardboard were stapled down, primed and then painted with two coats of Beckett

Blue emulsion. A 10cm (4in) brush covered the area quickly and one hour was allowed between coats. When the second coat was dry the floor was sealed with two layers of acrylic varnish; again, an hour's drying time was allowed between coats.

Furniture and fittings

Bunk beds are a sensible choice for two children sharing a room. Not only are they a great way to save space, they also appeal to them because they can double as a den, pirate ship or anything they care to imagine. Linda suggested self-assembly beds, which were ideal as the pieces could be painted bright blue before they were put together, to match the floor and accessories. To add a touch of individuality MDF flower and cockerel motifs were added to the bedposts and painted the same colour.

Improved storage was high on Linda's list of targets, and the twin alcoves either side of the chimney breast were an obvious place for cupboards. However, she felt the children would respond better to

something a little more exciting than run-of-the-mill cupboard doors. In keeping with the garden theme, the idea of two picket gates to fence off storage areas seemed a great alternative. Each gate was made from seven lengths of 1.8 x 12.5cm (¾ x 5in) timber. The central post was the highest and the others graduated down in height symmetrically. Using a paper template and a jigsaw, the tops of the posts were cut into rounded

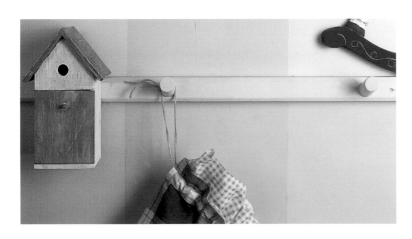

above Space was put to good use, even on the ceiling, where a big MDF collar, hung with a variety of interesting items, surrounded the light fitting.
below Small toys were kept in order in brightly coloured bags hung from a Shaker-style peg rail.

shapes and sanded. Then, for the horizontal back supports, two pieces of 6 x 2.5cm (2½ x 1in) finished timber were cut to the width of the alcove less about 1cm (½in) for the hinges. The vertical posts were laid evenly across the two horizontals, drilled and screwed together with countersunk screws. Then a crossways batten was cut to fit diagonally between the supports and secured with screws from the front. Once the holes were filled the gate was primed and painted. After an hour it was protected with a coat of acrylic varnish and left to dry. Finally the latches and hinges were fixed to mounting blocks and then to the gate.

A peg rail takes up next to no space, but with drawstring bags to hang from it offers lots of storage space, ideal for small toys like figures, dolls' accessories or bricks, which are invariably left on the floor to get trodden on or lost. Linda's was painted to match the walls and she added a little treasure drawer in the shape of a nesting box. The peg rail was easily contructed from a length of 5 x 5cm (2 x 2in) timber with holes drilled to hold pieces of 25mm (1in) dowelling. The dowelling was tapped into the holes with a mallet, and some glue was applied for extra strength before the edges were planed off and the rail painted. Using assorted scraps of fabric a variety of drawstring bags were simply made up, some with contrasting zigzag edging inserted along the lower hem to vary the look.

Dual-purpose items of furniture are always useful where space is limited.

Linda found a smart storage chest that would be perfect for the children's room as it can double as a bench. To incorporate it in the garden theme it was sanded, primed and painted. As a finishing touch, découpage motifs of insects and a snake were applied. These could be photocopies or images cut with sharp scissors from magazines or giftwrap paper. Border adhesive was used to stick the images on to the chest.

In children's rooms it's important to create as much novelty and interest as possible, so that there's something to amuse or inspire wherever they look. Ceilings are large areas with the potential for something eye-catching. Here, as the central light fitting was uninteresting, Linda surrounded it with a big circular MDF collar festooned with colourful, fun accessories. A piece of string was pinned on to a sheet of MDF, a pencil was tied to the other end to make a compass and a large circle was drawn. Then the string was shortened to allow another circle to be drawn about 20cm (8in) inside the first one. The collar was cut out, painted and small hooks were fitted at intervals. It was then attached to the ceiling with timber fixing-blocks and long screws fixed into the joists, ready to be decorated with fake vegetables, insects and flowers suspended from the hooks on cotton threads.

Window treatment

Blinds and banners are a clever way to create a striking window treatment without going overboard on the

below The garden theme included découpaged creatures roaming freely over the storage chest, and a painted MDF flower to brighten up the bedposts.

amount of fabric you need. Here, the blind was a dull, checked fabric and Linda came up with an easy and effective way to cheer it up, using fabric paints to print a small beetroot motif at regular intervals across the squares. She made her printing block by copying a motif from a paper pattern on to 3mm (⅛in) foam rubber and using a scapel to cut the foam. The foam motif was then glued with contact adhesive to a small timber offcut to make a printing block. To make the blind, the window was measured and two pieces of fabric,

5cm (2in) bigger all around, were cut and their right-side edges were sewn together leaving a small turning gap. The fabric was turned right-side out and, at regular intervals, two parallel lines of stitching were sewn from one side to the other to form a pocket. Lengths of dowelling cut to the same width were inserted in the pockets. Eyelets and cord were used to raise and lower the blind.

A pair of boldly checked fabric banners hung on either side of the blind gave the whole window area more presence. They were made by

above Wide, colourful, checked banners, hung either side of the window, gave the impression of a larger area and framed the cheerful hand-printed window blind.

hemming the tops of two widths of fabric and slotting them on to a slim, black metal pole. They were then finished off with fringed edgings, made from frayed lengths of woven fabric, which were stitched on to the remaining three sides of each of the banners.

Try this at home

It doesn't matter if you're less than expert with a drill, paintbrush or needle. You can confidently tackle these projects, from flooring to furniture. Read the instructions thoroughly first, have all the correct tools and components to hand and you're halfway there!

e, onde possa dimostrar quell

effetti Prego pero a V.S. o

non haura da desiderar mai

Painted walls

Stencilling, rag-rolling and other effects, which were so popular a few years ago have given way to fresher, more modern ways of using paint on plain walls. There are really no rules about what you can do, so, whatever your style, the range of colours, paint finishes and applied decoration now available should give you plenty of inspiration. Walls can be either the dramatic focus of a design, or the quiet backdrop for striking furniture, flooring or lighting. Paint treatments are currently replacing wallpapers as a versatile way of introducing pattern and variety into a scheme, opening up a vast pool of possibilities.

Painted wall stripes

Geometric patterns, like the stripes in Linda's design, might seem rather tricky to make as they won't look good unless they are very precise. If your hand is not the steadiest, don't worry. With the aid of masking tape you can create a quite complex and impressive effect using tonal horizontal stripes.

1 Paint the walls with the lighter paint tone as a base colour. When dry, use the pencil, long ruler and spirit level to mark out the first set of stripes. These should be broad, at least 30cm (12in) deep. Stick low-tack masking tape on the outer edges of these stripes and paint in with the darker shade.

2 Once dry, remove the tape. Choose one of the paler stripes at around shoulder height and, again with the spirit level, mark out a horizontal line that cuts this stripe in half. Stick masking tape above the pencil line. Make up a colour wash with the darker paint, diluting it with an equal amount of water, and apply it below the tape. You are aiming for a cloudy effect over each stripe of the paler base colour. The base colour stripes above the tape remain as they are. When dry, remove the tape.

3 With the pencil, ruler and spirit level, mark out the final stripe. This is a narrow one, about 5cm (2in) deep, above the top colour-washed stripe. Apply a strip of masking tape both above and below the narrow stripe, and then fill in with chrome spray paint. This tends to disperse more than ordinary paint, so two rows of tape are necessary to protect the walls. When dry peel off the tape.

1

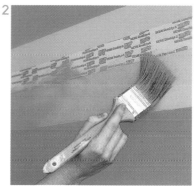

2

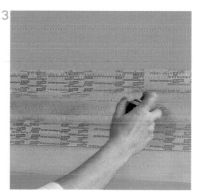

3

TOP TIP

Using darker colours nearer to the floor and lighter ones higher up will magnify the impression of height in a room. Vertical stripes have the same effect. Horizontal stripes increase the overall sense of space, leading the eye around the entire area.

Painted squares

It takes confidence to combine these bright colours so that they seem to jump and jar next to each other, but Laurence's design shows how successful the result can be. Use inexpensive match-pots to test a wide variety of colours you might not otherwise consider living with and, if you're feeling a little less than confident, you may find it helpful to plan the colour sequence on a sheet of paper before you begin. Aim for surprising contrasts and spirited combinations for a dramatic result.

1 Using the ruler, spirit level and pencil, draw a rectangle or square the size you want the finished design to be on to the wall. Divide it up equally into a grid of smaller squares, each of which should be a minimum of 14 x 14cm (6 x 6in). Fill in alternate squares with colour and, when these are completely dry, fill in the others. Masking tape is not necessary when using this method as none of the sides will bleed into any others, and the result will have a freehand, naïve feel. If you want a neater, more structured look, or feel your hand is a little unsteady, you will need to mask off alternate squares before painting, and then mask off the painted ones.

2 Add silver detailing to some squares at random, by first cutting a square of stencil card the same size as the painted squares. Cut a circle about 3cm (1¼in) in diameter, or a square about 12 x 12cm (5 x 5in) in the centre of the card. Hold the card slightly away from the painted square to be decorated and spray adhesive through the hole.

3 When the glue has become tacky but not too dry, carefully apply a piece of aluminium leaf to the square or circle with your finger, and brush away whatever does not adhere.

EQUIPMENT

MATERIALS AND

Ruler
Spirit level
Pencil
Emulsion or acrylic paint colours
Paintbrush
Low-tack masking tape (optional)
Stencil card
Scissors
Spray adhesive (e.g. Multi Mount from 3M)
Aluminium leaf

Freehand stripes and blocking

Geometric precision is not always necessary when you are making patterns. Here, Linda combined a hand-painted look with a sponge-stamped motif below the dado rail to give a relaxed feel with a unique element of character. If you don't have a dado rail, you can use a simple painted stripe to create the same impression.

1 Paint the walls with the base-coat colour and allow to dry. To paint the vertical stripes down from the dado rail, dilute the contrasting colour with water (2:1 paint to water) to ensure a fluid line. Using the artist's brush, start working on one section of wall and paint in the centre stripe. Add stripes on either side to quarter the area and then continue adding stripes in between these to build up the pattern. Then move on to the next section.

2 Once all the vertical lines are dry, make the first half of your stamp by cutting a decorator's sponge into a triangle. Tip a little of the contrasting emulsion colour on to a plate and dilute as before. Dip just the face of the sponge into the paint, and press this on to the edge below the dado at regular intervals. Try not to overload the sponge with paint as you will lose the mottled effect that is part of the look. Use the painted stripes as a rough guide for positioning your stamp.

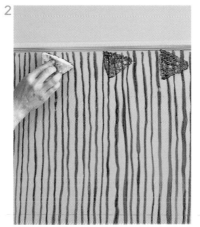

3 Make the second half of the stamp by cutting a sponge into a V-shape, checking that it is the right size to fit neatly between the stamped triangles. Use the same technique as before to apply the paint and allow to dry.

EQUIPMENT

MATERIALS AND

Emulsion paint: base-coat colour and contrasting colour

Paintbrush

Artist's fine brush

Decorator's sponges

Scissors

Old plate

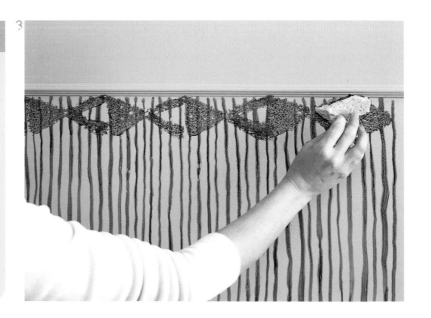

Polished plaster effect

The key to the success of Linda's polished plaster effect is the wonderful contrast of textures. The walls are bisected, allowing two different surfaces: matt paint below dado height and polished plaster above. This subtle surface with its delicate sheen looks sensational, but you will need some patience to achieve it.

1 Mark off the dado line with masking tape and paint the wall below with your chosen emulsion colour. Allow to dry thoroughly.

2 When the paint is dry, remove the masking tape and reposition it, aligning the top edge with the crisp edge of the paint, to keep the stucco plaster away from it. Mix the plaster following the manufacturer's instructions and apply the first layer with a wet trowel, tilting the bevelled edge of the trowel at an angle of about 30 degrees. Skim the plaster on in a smooth, thin layer and completely cover the wall above the tape. The plaster should not be more than 2mm (⅛in) thick. Allow to dry.

3 When the plaster is dry it will look pale and matt. Now apply a second thin layer of plaster on top of the first, using the same technique. Then take a dry trowel and, concentrating on an area about 1 metre (3ft) square, rework the wet plaster so that the surface becomes polished. The more pressure you put against the trowel as you work the greater the lustre you will achieve. Continue reworking the plaster in sections until the whole area has been done. (This stage is time consuming and a bit arduous, but the results are well worth the effort!) As the second layer dries out, the plaster will take on a mottled finish with a delicately shiny surface. Finally, carefully remove the masking tape. Show off the sheen with carefully positioned lighting or candles.

EQUIPMENT

MATERIALS AND

- Low-tack masking tape
- Matt emulsion paint
- Paintbrush
- Stucco plaster (e.g. Full Fat Cream from Ray Munn): to cover area above dado height,
- Plasterer's stainless-steel trowel

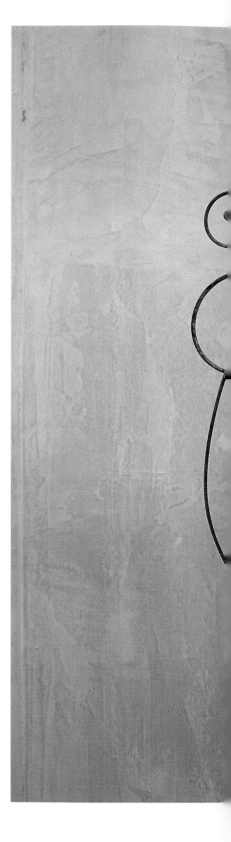

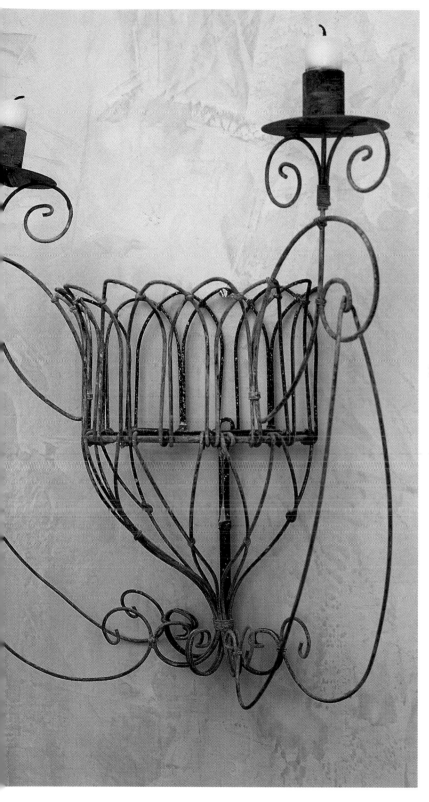

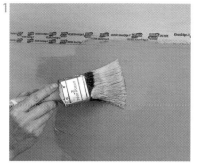

1

2

3

TOP TIP

This effect is all about contrasting matt and reflective surfaces. Colour takes second place, so choose your paint shade with care. Anything too obvious will detract from the subtlety of the plaster. A gentle neutral is the perfect foil for the clotted-cream look of polished plaster.

Plaster effect and calligraphy

Simple paint techniques can be used to give the flavour of an old Italian palace, mimicking rough, aged, plaster walls. Linda's subtle pattern of diamonds in gentle shades of pink, topped with traces of delicate, swirling script, creates interest without being overpowering. This scheme would make a relaxing backdrop for a living room or bedroom, teamed with soft shades of cream or deeper pinks.

1 First, create your background plaster effect. Paint the walls in the darker pink emulsion to give a flat finish. When this is dry, paint over roughly with the lighter pink shade to give a slightly mottled appearance.

2 When dry, mark out large diamond shapes in a row along the wall using the pencil and a long ruler or length of timber. They should extend from the floor to the picture rail. Paint in the diamonds with thinned white emulsion (2:1 paint to water) and an almost dry 4cm (1½in) paintbrush, so that the finished surface has an uneven, scrubbed look.

3 Find a suitable piece of calligraphy to copy on to the walls. Copyright-free books or old postcards are a good source. Take your chosen calligraphy to a copy bureau to be enlarged according to the wall space you want to cover and photocopied on to clear film. Place it on the overhead projector (these can generally be hired from a good art shop) and project the image on to the wall. You can then easily trace off the script using the artist's brush and thinned grey emulsion (2:1 paint to water). Try to keep a flowing, continuous motion, but don't worry if the lettering looks slightly wobbly as this will enhance the ancient, faded effect. Alternatively, you can enlarge the calligraphy on a photocopier and attach carbon paper to the back. To transfer the lettering to the wall trace over it with a pencil and then fill in the carbon copy with paint.

EQUIPMENT

MATERIALS AND

Emulsion paint: lighter and darker shades of plaster pink; white; grey

Paintbrush: size 4cm (1½in)

Pencil and artist's brush

Spirit level

Long ruler or length of lightweight timber

Calligraphy to copy

Overhead projector

Photocopier and carbon paper (see Step 3)

TOP TIP

If you want the script to be a focal point, opt for a few shorter lines, which will take up the middle area of a wall, from head to hip height.

Oriental
calligraphy

Anna's unusual and attractive border is extremely simple and easy to re-create. Look at oriental newspapers or local restaurant menus for inspiration for the lettering or, alternatively, the technique could readily be adapted to any type of calligraphy or motif. Painted in gold to complement a cream and red room, it creates a sumptuous effect.

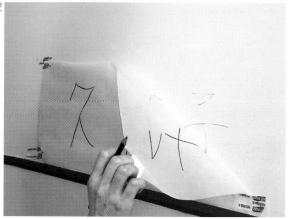

EQUIPMENT

MATERIALS AND

Oriental lettering to copy

Sheets of plain A4 paper

Pencil

Tracing paper

Masking tape

Gold or other metallic paint (e.g. from Plastikote)

Artist's soft brush

1 Once you've sourced your oriental lettering, copy your chosen characters on to a sheet of A4 paper in pencil, making each one about 12cm (5in) high. Use tracing paper to trace over the lettering, pressing hard enough to leave a slight impression on the A4 paper. Turn over both the A4 and the tracing paper and place the right side of the tracing paper exactly over the reversed impressions of the letters. Retrace the letters in pencil so that they are drawn and positioned identically on either side of the paper.

Turn back to the right side of the A4 paper and position it on the wall using masking tape. Run over the lettering again with a pencil.

2 Carefully lift off the tracing paper. The pencil lettering should now be faintly transferred on to the wall, to act as your guideline.

3 Use gold or other metallic paint and the artist's soft brush to define the tracings. Apply two coats if necessary. Try to work with a swift, emphatic brush stroke that will give a more authentic feel to the script, but don't worry too much about getting the lines perfectly straight. The idea is to create an impression of handwriting.

TOP TIP

Unless you're feeling very confident, choose simple characters without too many strokes close to each other, so that they look well defined when painted on to the wall. It may help to practise first on scrap paper to achieve a realistic-looking stroke.

Wall finishes

Paint is by no means the only medium for covering walls. You can bring texture and interest as well as colour to large spaces, using materials that may well surprise you at first. Aside from the usual DIY stores, trawl art shops and even garden centres and builders' merchants, where you can find some fabulously exciting and often inexpensive materials. Also be aware of new ways of using familiar components. Adopt an inventive approach, don't be afraid to experiment, and you will begin to create variety, and a truly original flavour in your home.

Fake wall panelling

Proper panelled rooms can look sensational, but unless you are lucky enough to have the real thing they are time consuming and expensive to re-create. This project uses ready-cut stick-on strips of beading from large DIY stores to mimic the look. The panels are a fixed size, but the way you space them out can have different effects on the mood of your room. Group them closely together for an ornate feel, while a looser arrangement will create a softer impression.

1 Using the spirit level, carefully mark on the wall where your fake panels are to go. Use the tape measure to make sure they are positioned evenly along the wall at regular intervals. Measuring and marking accurately is the hardest and most important part of the project, as the panels have to be perfect to look authentic.

2 The strips are ready-cut to size and the corners are mitred to fit snugly, so simply peel off the backing paper and stick the beading strips in place. As the kits are intended for livening up plain doors, you could include the door in your panelled design. You could also work wonders on drab wardrobe or cupboard doors.

TOP TIP

These panels are an invitation to add paint effects to a wall. For a subtle effect, paint the wall inside the beading slightly paler or darker than outside. Pick two contrasting colours for a dramatic effect, or experiment with picking out the beading in a different colour from the wall.

EQUIPMENT

MATERIALS

Spirit level with timber straightedge

Pencil

Tape measure

Self-adhesive beading strips ('Fake Victorian Door Panel Kit' usually used to spruce up plain doors)

Copper leaf decoration

The combination of metallic surfaces and candlelight is magical, so Linda's technique of burnishing a portion of wall with copper leaf is especially effective for a dining room, where you can create a theatrical environment for entertaining at night. The walls will quite literally glow, warming the whole room.

1 Using the spirit level, ruler and pencil, mark two straight lines on the wall to position the copper stripe.

2 Apply the stripe in sections. First, brush the size on to the wall in a block no more than 1m (3ft) square. Leave for approximately 30 minutes at normal room temperature, until it becomes tacky.

3 Apply the copper leaf, metallic side to the wall and with the backing paper facing you. Using the covered filler knife, rub really hard on the backing paper. The more time you spend rubbing, the better the burnished effect. Try to smooth out large creases but do not worry about tiny ones as they will add to the character of the finished result. Rub hard right up to the pencil edge so that you produce a neat, crisp finish. Carefully peel off the backing paper to reveal the leaf underneath. Repeat the process until the stripe is completed. As the overall finish is slightly uneven, don't worry about joins in the surface of the leaf; these won't be obvious.

EQUIPMENT

MATERIALS AND

Spirit level
Ruler
Pencil
Size (a special adhesive for gilding)
5cm (2in) paintbrush
Copper leaf
Filler knife with blade wrapped in soft cloth

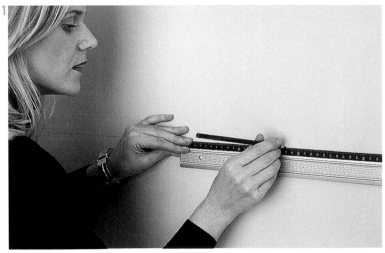

You don't need mirror-smooth walls for this technique. In fact, a slightly rough surface will bounce the light around more noticeably. Although primarily a wall finish, this idea can be translated to decorate accessories such as cupboard handles, while geometric groupings of copper squares can add style to cupboard doors.

When planning the position of your burnished stripe, take into account the location and level of lamps or a suitable shelf for candles. Adjacent lighting is crucial to make the most of the copper glow.

2

3

Fabric-lined walls

This spectacular tented effect is really not hard to achieve and requires little in the way of DIY skills. Fabric is an instant way to change the colour of a room, and Graham's technique is an excellent solution if your walls are in poor condition as it does away with time-consuming and tedious preparation. It's also an imaginative way of adding texture and interest to a room decorated in natural shades.

1 Cut lengths of battening with a saw to fit along the top and bottom edge of each wall and screw them in position. Fix further battens to the walls to make a series of frames to which to attach the fabric. You need to allow for doors, windows, sockets and other obstacles, so you end up with a variety of square and rectangular frames. *Note:* Take great care fixing battens near light switches or electrical sockets as there may be cables behind the plaster. To be on the safe side, glue the wood in these areas.

2 Measure each rectangle or square and cut a piece of fabric to fit, allowing 10cm (4in) extra all round. Starting at the top corner and working first along the top edge, fold under the raw edges and staple the fabric to the battens. Pull the fabric tightly down to the skirting batten, turn over the raw edges and staple in position. Attach the verticals next, starting in the middle of one side and working first downwards and then upwards. Ensure the tension is kept even throughout.

3 When the walls are totally covered cut eight to twelve lengths of fabric (depending on the size of the room) to dress the ceiling. The length of the pieces of fabric should be equal to the distance from the edge to the centre of the ceiling plus 1.5m (about 5ft). Fold under the raw edges towards you and staple the fabric to the battens at the tops of the walls. (Drape the bulk of the fabric over your shoulder to support it as you staple the edges.) Rather than pull the fabric taut across the ceiling, allow it to drape to give a tented effect. Tie the excess fabric in a loose knot in the centre of the room and secure it to the ceiling with staples.

EQUIPMENT

MATERIALS AND

Lengths of 2.5 x 1cm (1 x ⅜in) battening

Saw

3.75cm (1½in) Screws

Screwdriver

Glue (see Step 1)

Tape measure

Plain fabric (undyed dustsheets are an inexpensive option)

Scissors

Staple gun

Mirrored
pebbles-on-a-roll

Linda's unusual border scheme works especially well in a room inspired by natural elements as it allows the theme to be continued above eye level. The warm tones of the pebbles will echo polished floorboards, and the mirror details reflect and link different areas of the room. Caution: beware of sharp edges when cutting the mirror tile and wear safety goggles to protect your eyes from flying glass or pebbles.

1 Measure the perimeter of the room for the amount of pebbles-on-a-roll required and work out the number and position of the mirror insets you want. Spread out the pebbles-on-a-roll with the plastic backing uppermost and, with a pencil and ruler, mark out regularly spaced 8 x 8cm (3½ x 3½in) squares. Using a sharp craft knife cut out the squares from the sheet of pebbles. This is easier if you score diagonally across each square as well as around the edges.

2 Cut the mirror tile into 8cm (3½in) strips and then into squares. To do this, score the face of the mirror firmly once, holding the rotary cutter against a steel edge. Use the snapper part of the cutter to break the glass along the scored line.

3 Using the tape measure, pencil and spirit level, mark a guideline all around the room where you want the top edge of the pebbles-on-a-roll to be. Use panel adhesive to fix the sheet of pebbles to the wall in the required place. Then glue the mirrors into the cut-out squares using the same adhesive.

Tiled splashback

Tiling is nowhere near as complicated as you might imagine, and the principles involved are the same for a small splashback as for an entire bathroom wall. The golden rules are to prepare properly, ensure that you have the right tools and materials and not to rush the job.

EQUIPMENT

MATERIALS AND

Tiles: to cover the area of the splashback

Spirit level with timber straightedge

Ready-mixed or powdered tile adhesive

Adhesive trowel

Tile spacers: allow 2 per tile

Tape measure

Pencil

Tile scribe or tile-cutting tool

Ready-mixed or powdered waterproof grout

Damp cloth

Masking tape

Silicone sealant

Cartridge gun

Sharp knife

1 Clean and smooth the surface of the wall to be tiled, and loose-lay the tiles along the work surface at the bottom of it, checking with the spirit level that you are working along a straight edge. This will help you plan where to start.

2 Spread the adhesive on to the wall a little bit at a time with the adhesive trowel. Work section by section, six tiles at a time, and don't move on until everything is perfect. Press the tiles into place and, as you stick each one down, place a tile spacer at each corner so that every tile is evenly spaced from the ones that surround it.

3 At the point where a tile must be cut to fit, measure and mark very carefully before cutting. Always use a proper cutting tool to score and snap

1

2

3

TOP TIP
If your existing kitchen units need a bit of a facelift, you can easily tile down the wall and continue over the worktops as well. If the worksurface is a shiny plastic or formica-type finish, sand it down first to help the tile adhesive to bond.

the tile. If you are tiling a corner, use the piece you have just broken off to continue on to the next wall.

4 When all the tiles are in place, cover the area with waterproof grout, making sure it fills the gaps between the tiles. Quickly wipe off any surface grout with a damp cloth.

5 Put masking tape along the bottom of the tiled area where the tiling meets the work surface, then spread out a bead of silicone sealant with the cartridge gun to make this gap watertight.

6 Once the sealant is dry (about two hours but read the manufacturer's instructions), run a sharp knife along the top edge of the sealant and peel off the masking tape.

4

5

6

Sun mural

This mural looks very impressive,
but is surprisingly simple to do.

1 Have your sun image transferred on to clear film at a copy bureau. Using the overhead projector throw the image on to your plain wall and adjust its size and position.

2 Dilute a little grey emulsion with the same amount of water in a saucer. Using the artist's fine brush, carefully paint in the outline of the image. Build up the face of the sun with a combination of tiny dots and longer strokes. Leave to dry for about an hour.

3 Mix equal amounts of gold metallic powder and cellulose varnish to make a rich gold paint and fill in the sun's rays, using the artist's large brush. Allow about 15 minutes for it to dry. Clean the brush afterwards with cellulose thinner.

Cane wall cladding

Original ideas for decorating your home can come from absolutely anywhere. Garden centres are a source well worth investigating, especially for unusual textural and organic-looking materials which can be used in unexpected and highly effective ways. Graham's sensational wall cladding is relatively easy to construct and is made from ordinary, inexpensive garden cane.

EQUIPMENT

MATERIALS AND

Tape measure

Cane on a roll: about 1m (3ft) high, depending on the area you wish to cover

5 x 2.5cm (2 x 1in) battening, twice the length of the area to be clad.

Saw

Pencil

Drill with 6mm masonry bit; 3mm wood bit for pilot holes

Wall plugs to fit size 8 woodscrews

Hammer

Size 8 woodscrews

Screwdriver

Masking tape

Small-headed nails (tacks)

1 Measure the wall area to be covered and buy the necessary length of cane. Cut two lengths of battening to the length of the wall with a saw. Hold one length 10cm (4in) down from where you want the top edge of the cane roll to be and mark the position. Do the same with the other length, 10cm (4in) up from the bottom of the cane roll. Drill holes through the battens at about 40cm (16in) intervals with the 3mm wood bit, hold the battens up against the wall again and mark the positions of the holes on the wall. Drill holes into the wall as marked, using the 6mm masonry bit, tap the wall plugs in with a hammer and then screw the battens to the wall. These two parallel struts will form supports for the cladding.

2 Measure the length of cane roll required and saw off any excess.

3 Hold the cane roll in position against the battens and hammer small tacks through to fix it to the battens at regular intervals all the way along. To minimize splintering as the tacks go through the canes, stick a small piece of masking tape over the cane at each fixing point.

Floors

The floor is one of the largest surfaces in a room, and also one of the most often ignored, yet the potential beneath your feet is huge. Carpet or polished boards are by no means the limit. With less skill or cash than you might think, you can walk on something really special, either as part of your overall design or as a stunning focal point. Used imaginatively on floors, paint, fabric and other media can maximize the best and mask the worst aspects of a room, and add an extra dimension of colour, texture and substance to your space.

Timber floor border

Laurence's innovative idea for a floor border will revitalize a tired room or a carpet that has become grubby or damaged at the edges. It's also a much cheaper way of giving a room a new lease of life than splashing out on expensive new floor coverings. Because you can adjust the size of the border to suit your space, it lets you make use of less expensive carpet offcuts that may not exactly fit the dimensions of your room.

1 Clear the room, including the carpet, and then mark out a line on the floor all the way around, about 90cm (3ft) from the walls. Keep the lines parallel to the walls, even if the corners are not perfect 90-degree angles. Measure the length of the walls from corner to corner and then cut the floorboards that will be positioned nearest the walls accordingly with a handsaw or jigsaw. Use a mitre block to mitre the ends of each board where they meet at the corners. Do not assume every corner is a right angle, but check with a sliding bevel before cutting. Cut and secure each board in place only after you have fixed the previous one. This will ensure that your mitred corners line up exactly.

2 Working from the wall into the room, glue and then nail the first line of floorboards into place against the walls, using plenty of glue along the ends of each plank and in all the grooves.

3 To disguise fixings, nail the boards down through the tongues at about 15cm (6in) intervals, driving the nails in at an angle that will not obstruct the next board slotting into place. The groove of the adjacent board will hide the nails.

4 Once the wooden surround is in place apply a coat of acrylic varnish to seal and protect it, allowing at least two hours' drying time. Measure the length and width of the gap remaining in the centre of the room and cut your carpet to fit with the carpet knife. Hold the carpet in position with either double-sided carpet tape or nailed gripper strips.

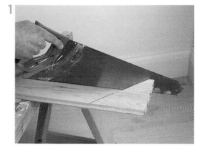

TOP TIP

If your hammer is not the right shape, use a nail punch to drive your angled nails right down into the wood (Step 3).

Colour-washed floorboards

Fabulous floorboards may lie beneath even the most hideous carpet, so it's always worth having a look at what's there. The boards can be sanded and sealed with varnish, or can be colour-washed before sealing. A patchy surface is no problem as the sander will cut through old varnish and dirt to bring all the boards up the same colour.

1 Clear the room and check the whole floor carefully for loose boards. These should be screwed firmly down. Remove or hammer down any protrusions like staples or projecting nail heads to produce a perfectly smooth and solid surface.

2 Use a combination of the large and hand-held sanders to smooth off the floorboards. Start with the large sander and work across the grain with coarse and then medium sandpapers. Finish off along the grain with the fine sandpaper.

3 Use the smaller hand-held sander to sand around the edge of the floor, using the same technique.

4 Mix your chosen emulsion colour with an equal amount of water and then brush it quickly on to the floorboards along the grain. Colour-washing allows the natural grain of the timber to show through, but the more water you add the paler and subtler the finished result will be. You may want to test different dilutions on a piece of scrap timber to give you an idea of the final look before washing over the whole area. Once painted, allow the floor to dry for an hour, then apply two coats of acyrlic varnish.

1

2

3

TOP TIP

For a bleached-effect floor, sand boards and paint with dilute white acrylic primer (see p 110: Graham's turquoise bedroom). To produce mock-grained floorboards rock a woodgraining rocker over wet glazed boards. Both these techniques can be applied to any other flat wooden surface, like a table top.

4

EQUIPMENT

MATERIALS AND

Screwdriver

Woodscrews

Claw hammer

Nail punch (optional)

Large and hand-held floor sanders

Coarse-, medium- and fine-grade sandpapers

Emulsion paint

Paintbrushes

Acrylic varnish

Stencilled floor 'rug'

Flamboyant fuchsia set against matt black makes Laurence's 'rug' a stunning way to add interest if carpeting a large area is beyond your budget. You will, however, need to do a bit of preparation if your floorboards are in poor condition. You may even have to invest some expense and time in hiring a sander if the surface is particularly tatty, but a little time spent doing thorough preparation will mean that you get a good, clean finish to this sensational painted floor technique.

1 If your floorboards are in poor condition, start by filling holes, securing any loose boards and sanding the whole floor to create a smooth, solid surface (see Colour-washed floorboards, p 156). Good preparation is vital if you want a clean finish to your painted floor, so it's worth spending time on this. Then taking into account the shape and dimensions of your room, and the positions of any items of furniture that might obscure your design, use a long ruler and pencil to mark out a large square or rectangle where you want to site your trompe l'ocil rug. Stick masking tape around the inside edge of the outline and then paint the area around the 'rug' black. When this is dry, protect the outside edge, again with masking tape, and fill in the centre panel with fuchsia. To create the narrow black border, use the ruler to mark out a stripe about 3cm (1in) wide and about 6cm (2in) in from the edge of the fuchsia panel. Stick masking tape down either side of the stripe, keeping the edges absolutely straight, and fill with black paint.

2 When the paint has dried, carefully remove the masking tape to reveal the border. Then trace out a flowing freehand design that overlaps the border of the 'rug'. Practise first on scrap paper then draw the design on to the floor with a pencil. (Look in art books if you need inspiration.) Add interest and depth to the design by varying the width of the lines you use.

3 Fill in the lines with an artist's brush and black emulsion. Although ideally you need a steady hand and a continuous sweep, don't worry if your painting is less than perfect. It will be far enough away from most people's eyes not to matter. When all the paint is dry, protect your design with two coats of acrylic varnish and leave to dry for at least 24 hours.

1

2

3

EQUIPMENT

MATERIALS AND

Long ruler
Pencil
Emulsion paint in black and fuchsia
Low-tack masking tape
Artist's paintbrush
Acrylic floor varnish

Fake flagstone floor

Real stone flooring may be your ideal but it's by no means an inexpensive choice, especially for a room of any size. The weight of stone can also cause problems if the joists below are not substantial enough. This project gives you an alternative to the real thing that won't break the bank or your foundations.

1 Clear the room and sweep the floor completely clean of all dust and debris. The surface must be absolutely solid before you start, so if yours is not a concrete floor it will need to be covered with hardboard. For this, measure the area, then lay down hardboard sheets, cutting them to size if necessary with a handsaw or jigsaw and securing them every 15cm (6in) with panel pins. Mix up a batch of self-levelling floor compound following the manufacturer's instructions and, working from the far end of the room towards the door, pour it evenly over the floor.

2 Use the plasterer's trowel to spread out the compound but don't try to smooth the surface too evenly as you will lose the natural stone-like quality you want to imitate. A few marks and a little unevenness will add character. Also, as the name suggests, the compound will level out of its own accord. The whole area must be covered in one session to avoid lines forming through the surface and spoiling the effect.

3 After one to two hours, depending on the air temperature, lay scaffolding planks on the floor to walk on and use either a stick or the edge of the trowel to score imaginary flagstones into the compound. Squares of about 30 x 38cm (12 x 15in) will give an authentic look. When the compound is firm enough to walk on, but not completely set, rescore the lines. If the floor is going to get a great deal of wear and tear, it is a good idea to protect it with a few coats of acrylic varnish. It will be more resilient to foot traffic and mopping up spills will also be easier. If the colour of the compound looks too dull, you can also paint it with emulsion before you varnish, which will add a further layer of protection.

Woven floorcloth

Making your own floor coverings is cost-effective and well worth the effort. The woven finish of Linda's mat looks very chic yet the upholstery tape from which it is made is extremely durable. Its natural colouring makes it the perfect accessory, bringing a touch of softness to a polished wooden floor.

1 Place the canvas cloth on the floor area to be covered and cut it to size. Measure the length and width of the cloth and cut pieces of the natural upholstery tape to equal the length and width of the canvas. Cut four pieces of black tape to equal the length of the cloth. Start weaving the natural tapes on top of the cloth by pinning a piece of tape the width of the cloth at a corner to lie horizontally across the cloth. Pin another piece of tape, the length of the cloth, from the same corner to lie vertically.

2 Pin a second pair of tapes to the canvas, weaving them up and over the first pair. Continue adding tapes in the same way, keeping the canvas flat and the tapes taut to ensure that the weaving is regular. The more tapes you add, the more involved the weaving becomes, so it's helpful at this stage to have two pairs of hands to avoid the weaving becoming distorted. To add interest, make the ninth and twelfth vertical tape from each side a length of contrasting black tape. This will give a pattern of broken 'tramlines' on each side of the mat, adding definition to the finished design. When the weaving is complete, machine-sew the outer edges to the canvas with canvas thread, keeping the cloth as flat as possible. Remove the pins.

3 To bind the raw edges securely, cut a length of tape for each side. Spread adhesive all over one side of each strip and allow to dry. Around the edges of the woven side spread a thin line of adhesive, half the width of the tape. When dry, bond half the width of the tape to the cloth. Turn the sides of the cloth over and spread a similar amount of adhesive around the edges of the underside. When dry, fold the tape over and bond as before. Trim the corners neatly to finish off.

EQUIPMENT

MATERIALS AND

Heavy-duty canvas cloth
Scissors
Tape measure
Hessian upholstery tape: natural and black
Pins
Sewing machine
Canvas thread
Contact adhesive

Windows

While conventional curtains still have their place, there are other easy and inexpensive ways to update and revitalize windows. Contemporary design has embraced current trends like the mixing of solid and sheer components together, and alternatives to fabric such as plastics. Blinds, made from a range of materials, now offer either a modern or traditional flavour and shutters are fast becoming yet another option. Fittings such as curtain poles and pelmets have assumed their own importance, taking on a variety of styles and finishes and now meriting as much attention as the window coverings themselves.

Laminated paper blind

Modern design has embraced all kinds of unconventional materials in recent years, and window treatments are no longer restricted to fabric and wood. Linda's out-of-the-ordinary blind is made from Chinese 'lucky papers'. They were bought very cheaply in books of about fifty from a Chinese supermarket, and were enclosed in clear plastic wallets.

EQUIPMENT

MATERIALS AND

Tape measure

Lucky papers

A4 laminating pouches and laminating machine (or go to a copy bureau)

Scissors

Nylon fishing line, paper clips, split metal rings or metal links cut from a chain

Hole punch or needle

5 x 2.5cm (2 x 1in) timber battening: the width of the window

Saw

Pencil

Drill

Wall plugs to fit size 8 screws

Hammer

Size 8 screws

Adhesive hook-and-loop strip (Velcro)

TOP TIP

The 1960s feel to this blind sets a funky tone that would be ideal for a kitchen with retro influences. It is also very practical as the wipe-clean surface is easy to maintain and allows light to flood in.

1 Measure the window so that you can calculate how many laminating pouches are needed to cover it. Laminate the lucky papers, either yourself or ask a copy bureau. Then trim all of them to the same size with sharp scissors, leaving a 1cm (½in) border of clear laminated plastic around each lucky paper.

2 Count the number of laminated papers needed for the drop and fasten these together in one length. If you have chosen to join them with fishing line, paper clips or split metal rings, use a needle to punch a hole through each corner of the plastic and pass the fastening through. Use a hole punch if you have chosen metal chain links as they will need larger holes. Fasten the lengths of laminated paper to each other in the same way to form the width required.

3 Saw the batten to the width of the window, position it either above the window or inside the recess and mark where the screws will go. Drill holes in the batten and the wall. Tap the wall plugs into the wall with the hammer and then screw the batten into place. To hang the blind, cut the Velcro strip into 10cm (4in) lengths and stick one length to each pouch along the top of the blind, ensuring that the lucky paper at the front covers the strip. Peel the backing off the strips, position the blind and press the strips against the batten.

Copper bead curtains

Laurence's inexpensive treatment brings great presence to a small window and can be put in over an existing plain blind. The gentle sheen of copper is the perfect partner for dramatically dark-coloured walls and also creates an effective contrast against sheer fabric. The wonderful flowing quality of muslin makes it the perfect fabric to use as it gives a light, airy feel to the room. Be lavish with it for a luxurious look.

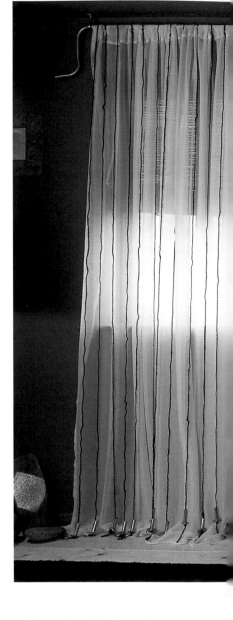

EQUIPMENT

MATERIALS AND

- String to determine length of pole
- 15mm (¾in) copper piping
- Hacksaw
- Masking tape
- Plumber's pipe bender
- White muslin
- Dressmaker's scissors
- Iron
- Sewing machine
- Power drill and masonry bit
- Wall plugs
- Small hammer
- Copper piping brackets (two per rail)
- Copper screws (two per bracket)
- Small or power screwdriver
- Rough sisal string
- Hand-wash dye (e.g. Black)
- Small block of modelling clay
- Copper aerosol spray paint
- Needle and thread
- Spray lacquer or varnish

1 To determine the length of your copper-piping curtain pole take a piece of string and follow the proposed shape of the rail on the wall. You will need to allow extra piping for the pieces used in Step 6. Hold the piping for the pole steady on a workbench and cut off the required length cleanly with the hacksaw.

2 Use small pieces of masking tape to mark where the brackets will be fixed on the piping. Then use a plumber's bender to create the unusual bends. Insert it into one end of the piping and bend at the point where one of the pieces of masking tape is, to make a 90-degree angle. Repeat the process nearer the end of the piping, bending it back in the other direction to make an S-shape. Do the same at the other end.

3 Each curtain is made from a single width of muslin, but if your windows are wide, join two or more widths together. The drop is the floor to ceiling measurement plus another 20cm (8in) for generous bunching up on the floor. Cut and press the fabric.

4 Fold a 2.5cm (1in) hem over and sew to close the turned edge with a running stitch. Fold a similar double hem at the top of the curtain, allowing a 5cm (2in) turn. Sew as

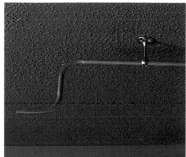

before. Pass the copper rail through the channel created by the top hem on the fabric. Drill and wall plug fixing holes and screw copper brackets into the ceiling above the window. Hang the rails from the brackets.

5 Cut sisal string into lengths sufficient to run down from the curtain pole and lie on the floor. Dye the string with the hand-wash dye according to the manufacturer's instructions and allow to dry in an airing cupboard (drying can be speeded up with a hairdryer).

6 Make round, coin-like beads from the clay. These will dry in about four hours. Spray the beads with copper paint, thread one bead on to the end of a knotted length of string and then thread a 5cm (2in) piece of copper pipe on top of the bead. Protect the bead and copper pipe with lacquer or varnish. Make enough beaded strings to decorate the curtain and then sew them to the curtain top. Add hooks and tiebacks made from dyed string if required.

Personalized pelmet

All that bunched-up fabric at the top of curtains can sometimes make them look unfinished. A pelmet is the neatest disguise and can be a feature in its own right. This simple wood or MDF construction gives you scope to use your imagination.

1 Measure the width of the window and add 15cm (6in) at each end to give you the length of the front panel. The height of the panel will depend on the design you have in mind but about 20cm (8in) works well for a simple curving shape. Cut the front and side panels from the MDF or plywood with the jigsaw. The depth of the side panels can also vary according to your design, but should be the same height as the front for a continuous frame around the top of the window. Cut two battens to the height of the pelmet and make pilot holes using the 3mm wood bit for the drill, or the bradawl. Apply wood glue and use the 3cm (1¼in) screws to screw the battens along each end of the front panel.

2 Attach the side panels to the front-panel battens in the same way, putting the screws through from the back to avoid screw-head marks.

3 Draw your decorative edge design on the paper and cut it out to use it as a template, or alternatively draw directly on to the front panel edge. Cut along this line with the jigsaw and sand off any rough edges.

4 Use the finished pelmet as a guide to mark out positions for two timber wall battens, which will fit inside the side panels of the pelmet. The centre point of these battens should align with the top of the window. Use the spirit level to check they are straight, mark pilot holes in the wall with the bradawl or using the drill and the 3mm wood bit. Then drill holes into the wall with the 6mm masonry bit, put in the wall plugs and screw the battens to the wall using the 4cm (1½in) screws.

5 Hold the pelmet up to the wall so that the wall battens fit inside and align with the side panels. Fix the battens to the pelmet sides with wood glue and 3cm (1¼in) screws, working from inside the pelmet.

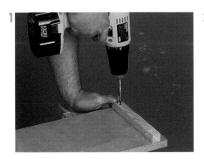

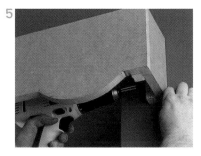

TOP TIP

Decorate the pelmet before you fix it into place. Use a flat coat of paint, a paint effect or even a fabric wrap. The pelmet can match or contrast with your curtains depending on the look you want.

Stencilled blind

Stencilling a blind is as easy and straightforward as stencilling on to a wall, and is a great way to turn a plain window treatment into something special. Linda's design of lemons and leaves will bring a bold, fresh look to a kitchen but you can adapt the technique to create motifs to suit any room in your home.

1 Draw or trace your stencil design on to a sheet of stencil card, using any images you like. Look in magazines, books or any copyright-free source for inspiration, or just invent your own. Bear in mind that a symmetrical motif will work best positioned centrally on a blind, but you could use a border design as an alternative. Shade in the parts of the design that will be cut away to allow the paint through. Remember to leave solid parts too, so that your stencil does not fall apart.

2 Place the card on a suitable cutting surface such as an old lino offcut and carefully cut out the shaded parts of the design using a sharp craft knife. Place the blind on a work surface and use a little masking tape or spray adhesive to hold the stencil in position on the blind.

3 Using a stencil brush, apply water-based acrylic paints through the stencil. Work with a light, stippling motion to achieve a broken, almost hand-painted effect. Resist the temptation to lift the stencil before you have filled in every part, as you may not be able to reposition it in exactly the same place.

EQUIPMENT

MATERIALS AND

Stencil card
Pencil
Tracing paper (optional)
Images
Cutting surface
Craft knife
Masking tape or spray adhesive
Stencil brush
Water-based acrylic paints

TOP TIP

Stencilling is not a new technique, but it remains popular because it is so simple and effective. For a contemporary look steer clear of small, fussy motifs and go for a large, bold style.

'Copper'-style curtain pole

The market is awash with curtain poles of all designs, but they can be expensive. Linda's design follows the modern trend for metallics but won't break the bank.

1 Clamp the pole in a vice and cut it to the required length. Drill a hole in either end to a depth of 2.5cm (1in). (The drill bit should be a little smaller than the diameter of the pole.)

2 Cut the copper wire into 12cm (5in) lengths with the wire cutters and gather into bundles large enough to fill the holes you have drilled. Spray the pole, and the wires if you are using garden ones, with copper spray paint. Spray the curtain rings and wall brackets with the same paint and leave everything to dry thoroughly. Half-fill the holes at either end of the pole with silicone sealer and push in a bunch of copper wires, keeping all the ends even. Allow the

sealer to dry and harden so that the wires are firmly held. Then spray everything, including the wires, with a coat of polyurethane varnish and leave to dry. Finally, measure and mark the position of the brackets on the wall. Drill holes and plug the wall with the wall plugs, then screw the brackets in place. They should hold

the pole 25cm (10in) proud of the window. Attach the pole to the brackets and fan out the wires at the ends to make a striking finial shape.

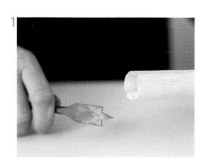

Gilded shutter mirrors

When the shutters are closed at night Linda's gilded glass panels softly reflect light from inside the room.

1 Use the paintbrush to splatter the glass panels with a mixture of white polish and spirit-based wood dye. This dries in about 20 minutes. Then spray the glass with adhesive and apply découpage images right-side down on top of the splattered surface. Spray with adhesive again, then press Dutch metal leaf over the découpaged surface to cover the whole area of the glass.

2 Dry-brush away the excess Dutch metal leaf and leave for two hours to dry. Protect with spray polyurethane varnish and leave to dry for a further hour. When dry, secure the gilded side of the mirrors to the shutters with panel adhesive. At night the layers of splatters and découpage will show through with the metal leaf behind them.

TOP TIP

Shutters make an attractive alternative to curtains but, when closed, give a restricted feel. Shiny glass, enhanced by gilding, will introduce a pool of light, breaking up a heavy block and adding a sense of the outside beyond.

EQUIPMENT

MATERIALS AND

7.5cm (3in) paintbrush

Glass panels: cut to size to fit shutter rebates

White polish (clear polish mixed with white wood dye)

Spirit-based wood dye, e.g. Dark Oak

Spray adhesive

Découpage images (from copyright-free book)

Dutch metal leaf: to cover area of glass

Brush

Polyurethane spray varnish

Panel adhesive

Ornamental
curtain pelmet

The way we live today puts pressure on furniture to serve several functions.
Sometimes you need a permanent screen, sometimes just a temporary measure
that makes more flexible use of your space. This combination of solid pelmet
and movable curtains can close off part of a room and is the ideal solution.

1 Measure MDF or plywood pelmet panels high enough to accommodate your intended design (about 46cm (18in) is a workable size) and wide enough to span the width of the room. Cut to size with the jigsaw. Use a paper template to make a full-size motif for the repeating pattern along the pelmet and then trace around it so that you create an evenly spaced design along the entire length of MDF. Jigsaw out the final shape.

2 Using wood glue and 3cm (1¼in) screws, attach lengths of the 5 x 2.5cm (2 x 1in) timber batten to the back of the MDF panels to join them into one complete pelmet. Check that it fits the room span exactly.

3 Attach a 2.5 x 2.5cm (1 x 1in) timber batten all along the top edge of the pelmet with glue and 3cm (1¼in) screws and allow to dry.

4 Hold your finished pelmet up in position and use the 3mm drill bit to create pilot holes in the timber batten and marks for the plugs in the ceiling at the same time. The pelmet will need to be secured at intervals of about 15cm (6in) to support the weight. Remove the pelmet and drill

TOP TIP
For a long room, install twin pelmets back to back and combine them with a pair of screens instead of curtains for a temporary room-divider.

the ceiling where the marks are using the 6mm bit. Insert cavity wall plugs or self-drill plasterboard fixings. Finally screw through the battens into the ceiling to secure the pelmet in place using 4.5cm (1½in) screws. Your curtains can either be attached to the back of the pelmet using curtain track, or to a rail fixed behind it. If you plan to paint your pelmet the same colour as the ceiling or walls, you can do this once it is fitted up. If it will be a different colour, it is advisable to paint it beforehand.

EQUIPMENT

MATERIALS AND

Tape measure

Pencil

1.25cm (½in) MDF or plywood: enough to span the room and drop 46cm (18in)

Jigsaw with timber-cutting edge

Paper for template

Drill with 3mm wood bit for pilot holes; 6mm masonry bit

Wood glue

Woodscrews: 3cm (1¼in) size 8; 4.5cm (1¾in) size 8

Screwdriver or screwdriver bit for drill

5 x 2.5cm (2 x 1in) timber: enough for upright battens on back of pelmet

2.5 x 2.5cm (1 x 1in) timber: enough for horizontal battens on back of pelmet

Cavity wall plugs or self-drill plasterboard fixing plugs: enough for one every 15cm (6in) of span

1

2

3
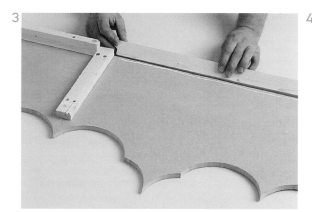

4

Chalet shutters

These Swiss-style shutters make a refreshing change from curtains. They use up a fairly substantial amount of timber but the results make it well worth the expense.

TOP TIP

The added beauty of this project is that the shutters can be made for windows of any size. Why not try making them for a pair of patio doors? The construction technique is exactly the same.

1 Measure the height and width of the window, then calculate the dimensions for two equally sized shutters to fit the space. They should be no wider than about 80cm (32in) each, so if your window is more than about 1.6m (5ft) wide you will need four shutters instead of two. Cut 10cm (4in) tongue-and-groove planks with a saw to make the shutters and fit each shutter together by gluing down every groove to make a solid panel. Leave to dry for two hours.

2 On what will be the inside of each shutter, create a bracing Z-shape from the 7.5 x 2.5cm (3 x1in) planed timber to add strength and rigidity to the doors. Use wood glue and 4cm (1½in) size 8 woodscrews to fix the two horizontal braces in position about 15cm (6in) from the top and bottom of the shutter.

3 Measure and mitre the diagonal battens using a sliding bevel so that they fit against the horizontal battens. Secure using the same method. Be tidy – this side will be visible when the shutters are open.

4 Measure and cut two vertical battens from the 2.5 x 2.5cm (1 x 1in) timber for the wall on either side of the window. They should be exactly the same height as the shutters, that is, the height of the window. Fix the battens in position. Use the spirit level to check they are straight and mark pilot holes in the wall with the bradawl or using the drill and the 3mm wood bit. Then drill holes into the wall with the 6mm masonry bit, put in the wall plugs and screw the battens to the wall using 5cm (2in) size 10 woodscrews. These battens will be taking the entire weight of the shutters. They will be particularly under strain near the top, so should be attached to the wall every 15cm (6in). If in any doubt, upgrade to 5 x 2.5cm (2 x 1in) battens and add more screws.

5 Screw a pair of 23cm (9in) T-hinges to the unbraced side of the shutters (the first two only, if you are making four shutters) about 15cm (6in) from the top and bottom of the shutters. Use 1cm (½in) size 8 woodscrews and make sure they do not show through on the other side.

6 Screw the two shutters by their hinges to the wall battens using 2.5cm (1in) size 8 woodscrews. If you are making four-panel shutters, use four more T-hinges to attach the third and fourth ones, placing the hinges on the braced side so that the shutters fold in on themselves when opened.

Harlequin shutters

Linda's shutters are designed to allow light into the room without the need to open them. The open panels are covered with sheer muslin for privacy.

EQUIPMENT

MATERIALS AND

Tape measure

Pencil

7.5 x 2.5cm (3 x 1in) timber: enough to make horizontal sections of shutters.

5 x 2.5cm (2 x 1in): enough to make the upright sections of shutters

3mm (⅛in) MDF: enough to fill in centre panels of shutters

Router

Wood glue

Panel pins

Mitred moulding lengths: enough to surround each panel

Drill with 10mm wood bit

Jigsaw

Medium-grade sandpaper

Cotton muslin fabric to cover open panels

Hand-wash dye (e.g. Lilac)

Iron

Scissors

Staple gun

Braid (between 5 and 10mm in width)

Hot-melt glue gun

5cm (2in) flush hinges

Magnetic catches

1 Measure the window frame and divide into thirds. The two wider shutters are equal to a third each and the two smaller ones are each half of the remaining third. Make a wide and a small shutter frame for each side, using the 7.5 x 2.5cm (3 x 1in) timber for the horizontals and the 5 x 2.5cm (2 x 1in) timber for the uprights. Use MDF to fill in the open centres.

2 Rout the timber frames at the edges to fit the MDF. Secure the MDF to the frames with wood glue and finish neatly by panel-pinning lengths of mitred moulding around the MDF. Allow two hours for the glue to harden.

3 Using a pencil, divide each MDF panel in half both vertically and horizontally. Join up the outer points to form diamond shapes top and bottom. Drill a pilot hole using the 10mm wood bit, insert the cutting blade of a jigsaw and cut out the diamond shapes. Smooth the edges with medium-grade sandpaper.

4 Dye 2m (7ft) of the cotton muslin with the hand-wash dye. When dry, iron the fabric and cut out panels. Staple these behind each diamond-shaped opening and cover the staples with braid secured with the hot-melt glue gun.

5 Hinge the screens into two matching pairs, then hinge the larger screens to the architrave around the window. Fit magnetic catches at the top and bottom of the smaller screens so that they close in the middle.

Checked blinds with decorative ties

Laurence's effective window treatment requires minimal sewing skills and looks sensational, particularly in a more traditional room. A bright, distinctive fabric, like the one Laurence has used here, will make the blinds a real feature and any leftover fabric can be used to re-upholster chairs for a coordinated look.

1 Hem the fabric and sew one side of Velcro along the top of the wrong side. Staple the other side of Velcro along the batten.

2 Screw the batten to the top of the window frame and fix an MDF box pelmet to conceal unsightly fixings at the top of the blind. If required, a strip of decorative moulding can be fixed to the pelmet with wood glue and panel pins.

3 Four ties hold the gathered blind just below the pelmet. To make each tie, cut a strip of blind fabric the same length as the window drop. Fold the edges to the inside along the length on both sides, then fold the strip in half and stitch to close. Staple two ties to the front of the blind and two to the back, each about 15cm (6in) in from the sides of the window. Tie each pair neatly.

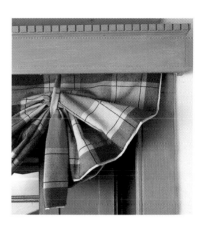

Furniture

Today's furniture is forging its own path, especially in terms of some of the industrial, raw-looking materials that are used. Making your own pieces may seem daunting but you could be pleasantly surprised by what you can achieve with the minimum of skill – and you will create something totally unique and personal for your home.

Beaded radiator cover

Radiators can be awkward to incorporate in a scheme but Linda's imaginative design, inspired by a radiator cover seen at Charleston, the gathering place of the Bloomsbury set in the early twentieth century, should spark some ideas. Of course, you can use the basic method shown here to act as a starting point for your own design. Remember, however, when formulating your ideas, that you must leave plenty of open space at the front so that air can circulate properly around the room.

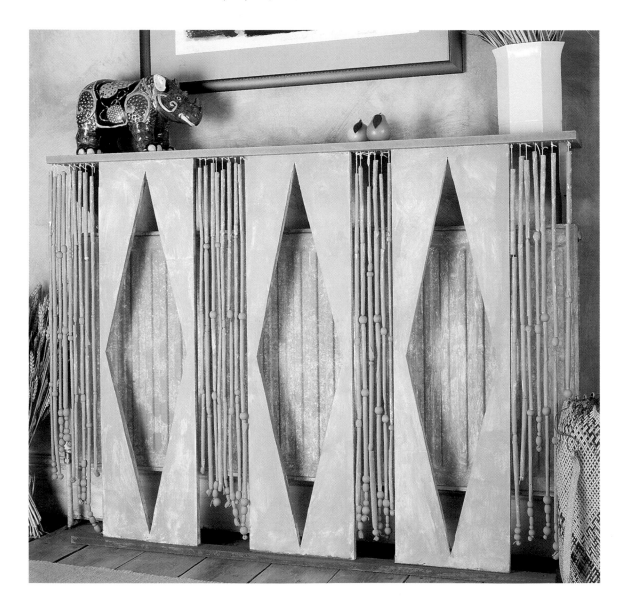

1 Make long cylindrical beads by wetting each paper strip with PVA glue. Wrap it around a drinking straw, then remove the straw and leave the paper to dry overnight. Make about 120 of these, then combine with about 120 of the wooden beads and put batches of beads into a plastic bag, pour in some emulsion and shake. Repeat until all the beads are coated. Leave to dry. Cut the string into pieces long enough to reach from the underside of the top of your planned radiator cover, almost to the floor (these will be longer than the

depth of the radiator). Thread enough strings to fill the gaps in the front, interspersing the paper beads with wooden ones. Measure two timber battens to the width of the radiator and cut with a handsaw or jigsaw. Fix one to the wall, leaving at least 5cm (2in) clearance at the top of the radiator for heat to circulate. Mark pilot holes with the bradawl or using the drill and the 3mm wood bit. Then drill holes into the wall with the 6mm masonry bit, put in the wall plugs and screw the battens to the wall. Use a spirit level to check that it is level.

2 Measure, cut (and paint if required) a shelf from 1.25cm (½in) MDF, the exact width and depth of your planned radiator cover, and attach it to the top batten with wood glue and screws.

3 Screw the second batten to the floor so that its front edge is at least 2.5cm (1in) forward of the radiator, again to allow air to circulate.

4 Cut three pieces of 2cm (¾in) MDF to make the front panels. They should fit exactly in the space between the floor and the underside of the shelf. Mark out a diamond shape on each panel and cut out with the jigsaw. To start the jigsaw off use the 10mm wood bit to drill a hole inside the area of MDF that is to be removed and use this to get the blade in.

5 Paint the panels. Use screws and wood glue to fix them to the underside of the shelf and the front of the floor batten – space them evenly across the radiator. Staple lengths of beads so that they hang in the spaces between the panels.

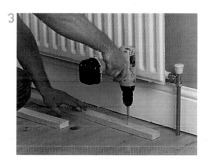

Alcove display unit

The ordinary way to deal with alcoves on either side of a fireplace is to fill them with shelves or fit a wardrobe or cabinet into the space. If you already have enough storage, Graham's design gives you a more original option, creating an unusual display feature for striking ceramics or sculpture. It can even be lit for maximum effect. If you like the technique, but don't have a fireplace, you can build the unit almost anywhere you like, as long as you have fixing points on the floor, ceiling and one side of any opening.

EQUIPMENT

MATERIALS AND

- Tape measure
- Pencil
- 2cm (¾in) MDF or plywood: about two 2.4 x 1.2m (8 x 4ft) sheets
- Drill with 3mm wood bit; 6mm masonry bit; 10 mm wood bit
- Jigsaw with timber-cutting blade
- Timber battens: 5 x 2.5cm (2 x 1in) to go all around alcove; 2.5 x 2.5cm (1 x 1in) to go all around each opening
- 6mm wall plugs (solid or cavity)
- 4cm (1½in) size 8 woodscrews
- Screwdriver; or screwdriver bit for drill
- Wood glue
- Paint

TOP TIP

If you plan to light your alcove, consult a qualified electrician. The shelf boxes must be shallower than the depth of the alcove to allow for wiring behind, with a translucent backing to let the light through. Bulbs will need changing, so the backing must be removable. Velcro tape will allow easy access.

1 Measure the height and width of the alcove and cut a sheet of MDF exactly to these measurements. Mark out a square on the MDF panel for the opening and cut out with the jigsaw. Drill a hole inside the area using the 10mm wood bit to start off the jigsaw. An opening about 30 x 30cm (12 x 12in) will make a practical display area but you can vary the size, and number of openings, depending on the size of the alcove.

2 Cut two 5 x 2.5cm (2 x 1in) timber battens to match the depth of the alcove and another two to match the width. Attach the long battens to either side of the alcove and the short ones to the top and bottom. Drill pilot holes in the wall with the 3mm wood bit. Then drill holes into the wall with the 6mm masonry bit, put in the wall plugs and screw the battens to the wall. You will not need plugs for the bottom batten if the floor is wood. Make sure all the battens are fixed exactly the same distance from the back of the alcove so that the unit is straight. Check that the large MDF panel rests snugly against the battens in the alcove.

3 Measure from the front of the battens to the back of the alcove and use this measurement, and the size of the cut opening, to make a square box from MDF with just four sides and no top or bottom. Joint the sides with glue and screws.

4 Cut lengths of 2.5 x 2.5cm (1 x 1in) timber batten to match the sides of the cut opening. Use these battens to attach the box to the front panel with glue and screws. Allow the glue to dry. The unit is now ready to be fixed into place. Drill some pilot holes through the main panel before securing it to the battens on the walls, ceiling and floor with glue and screws. The unit can now be painted.

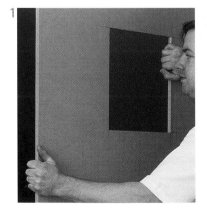

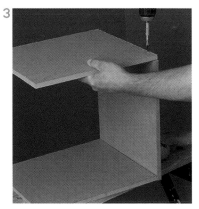

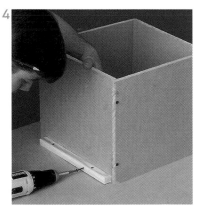

Bagel-shaped cabinet

The visual impact of an item of furniture is often as important as its practicality. A conventional kitchen wall-shelf is useful but lacks the dash of Linda's gorgeous bagel-shaped cabinet. Although very simple in form, it is so unusual that it becomes the focal point of the room. You can also echo the shape in other elements of the room: Linda painted large-scale bagel motifs on to a feature wall to complete the look.

1 Decide on the size of your cabinet and use the pencil and steel rule to draw lines for the straight top and bottom edges on to the MDF. Draw lines 12.5cm (5in) inside these. To draw the curved ends take a piece of wood at least 50cm (20in) long and drill a hole at one end. This will form the pivot of a simple 'pair of compasses'. Place the hole exactly between the ends of the two inside parallel lines, where the curve should start. Mark, and then drill, two holes in the centre of the wood at the position of the inside and outside lines. The two holes should be the same distance from each other as the lines are. Position the compasses on the MDF so that when a pencil is put through either hole and the wood is swung around the pivot, the pencil lines meet the top and bottom straight lines. When you are happy with this, hammer a nail through the pivot into the MDF and draw the inner and outer curves. Repeat for the other end and cut out the exterior shape with a jigsaw. Then cut carefully along the inner line, starting off just inside the line on the central area of MDF, which will drop out.

Sand the edges smooth and use this shape as a template to create the second bagel shape. These are the two formers (main parts) of the unit.

2 From the offcuts of MDF cut at least twelve pieces, each 12.5cm (5in) wide and about 25cm (10in)

long with a saw. These struts will separate the front former from the back one. Their length determines the depth of the unit, so choose a depth to suit your needs. With a pencil, mark the positions of the struts around one bagel shape. They should be about

MATERIALS AND

Pencil

Steel rule

Sheet of 12mm (½in) MDF

Piece of timber: about 50cm (20in) long

Drill

Nail

Hammer

Jigsaw with timber-cutting blade

Fine-grade sandpaper

Saw

Wood glue

Size 8 woodscrews

Screwdriver

Flexiply or FlexiMDF, approximately 4mm (¼in) thick

Nail gun or flat-headed nails (tacks) and hammer

Nail punch

Filler

Paint

5cm (2in) paintbrush

Mirror-fixing plates to attach the unit to the wall

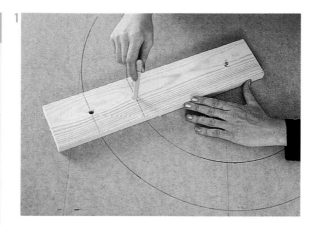

10cm (4in) apart around the curve and about 20cm (8in) apart on the straight sides. Drill two holes through each mark and into the end of each strut. Glue and screw each one into place. Once secure, fit the second former over the first, again using glue and woodscrews. Take great care that everything matches perfectly and that the shelf supports are absolutely symmetrical. Another pair of hands may be useful at this stage.

3 Once the glue has dried, measure the depth and circumference of the joined shapes and cut the Flexiply or FlexiMDF to fit. Using a nail gun or hammer and tacks, attach the strip

around the carcass at intervals of 7.5–10cm (3–4in). Work all the way around until you reach the starting point, where the ends should butt up perfectly. Measure around the inside edge, cut a further strip and attach it

in the same way. Sand all the edges both inside and out until smooth, depress the nail heads with a nail punch then fill, sand and paint the unit. When dry it can be hung on the wall with mirror-fixing plates.

Fretwork radiator cover

Precut fretwork panels are now readily available from most of the major DIY stores. They are available in a great range of designs, suggesting all kinds of decorative possibilities: the screening Graham has used here is called Jali fretwork. Graham's idea is perfect for masking a shabby radiator, especially in a formally styled room. For a smart overall effect, paint the whole cover in one shade and disguise the radiator by painting it black.

1 Measure the radiator and add 15cm (6in) all around for the valves on each side and for air to circulate. Mark these measurements on the MDF and cut out the rectangular piece with a jigsaw. This will make both the inner and outer frames of your cover, so cut carefully. First mark out a rectangle 5cm (2in) from the top and sides of the panel but 12.5cm (5in) from the bottom. Then draw a second rectangle 5cm (2in) inside this one. Carefully cut out the inner frame, first making a drill hole with the 3mm wood bit in which to start off the jigsaw blade.

2 Measure the distance the radiator projects from the wall and add 5cm (2in) to this. Mark out

the top and side panels of the cover to this width on the MDF and cut out with a jigsaw. Fix these panels to the outer frame with wood glue and screws to form the carcass of the cover. Cut four small MDF triangles for the backstops to the fretwork panel and glue and screw them, one behind each corner of the outer frame.

3 Cut the fretwork panel to a size 2.5cm (1in) smaller all around than the outer edge of the inner frame and fix it on to the back with glue and screws, checking that it is straight before finally screwing. Drill pilot holes for the screws to prevent splitting the fretwork.

4 To complete the carcass measure a length of skirting

board to fit around the three sides of the cover, flush with the bottom edge. You can create the mitre cuts quickly with a jigsaw or with a circular saw that can be locked in a 45-degree cutting position. Alternatively mark the skirtings with a pencil and use a handsaw. Use wood glue and screws to attach the skirting to the outer frame. Don't worry that it is higher than the bottom of the outer frame. In tandem with the small corner triangles this will form the slot in which the fretwork panel sits.

5 Fix some 5cm (2in) architrave around the top edge of the cover with glue and panel pins.

6 The fretwork panel should now sit between the edge of the

  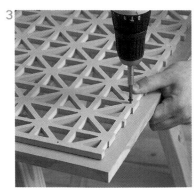

EQUIPMENT

MATERIALS AND

Tape measure

Pencil

2cm (¾in) MDF or plywood: approximately one 2.4 x 1.2m (8 x 4ft) sheet

Jigsaw with timber-cutting blade

Drill with 3mm wood bit

Wood glue

Woodscrews: 3cm (1¼in) size 8; 1cm (½in) size 6

Screwdriver; or screwdriver bit

Fretwork panel: to cover radiator

15cm (6in) Torus skirting board: to go around radiator cover

5cm (2in) Ogee architrave: to go around radiator cover

Circular saw or handsaw (optional)

Panel pins

Pin hammer

Nail punch

2 magnetic catches

skirting at the front and the MDF triangles at the back. Fix a couple of magnetic catches to hold it in place. The panel can easily be removed for access to the valves, and the cover is not fixed to the wall but simply rests on the floor.

4

5

6

Room-divider screen

Linda's screen is the ideal way to make your space work more flexibly for you, temporarily sectioning off larger or smaller areas as you require. It is also a great way to change a day room into an evening one, masking toys or a home office area. For evening entertaining, place a light on the floor behind the screen to make an attractive focal point.

1 Decide on the height and width of your screen and then cut three identical panels from the MDF or plywood. To make a semicircular shape at the top of each panel, use a piece of scrap timber or string and a pencil. Find the centre of the panel across its width and either nail in one end of the timber batten or anchor a piece of string with a nail. Using a pencil held at the free end of the batten or string, draw a semicircle at the top of the panel. Cut around the line with a jigsaw. If you want a more

EQUIPMENT

MATERIALS AND

Tape measure

Pencil

2cm (¾in) MDF or plywood: two 2.4 x 1.2m (8 x 4ft) sheets

Compass (optional) made from a 60cm (2ft) piece of scrap timber batten and a nail at least 4cm (1½in) long, or string and a pencil

Hammer

Jigsaw with timber-cutting blade

Paper for template (optional)

Six flush hinges or piano hinges and screws

Bradawl

Screwdriver

Decoration for screen

elaborate shape for the top of your screen, draw your design on to paper and cut it out to make a template. You can then draw around this on to the MDF to mark your cutting line, and cut with a jigsaw as before. Sand the cut edges smooth.

2 Screw three hinges to the edges of two panels to be joined, one in the middle and the other two 30cm (12in) from the top and bottom of the panels. Use the bradawl to make pilot holes. Remember to fit the hinges so that the panels fold in alternate directions, like a zigzag. The screen can then be decorated as you wish, for example with paint, paper, fabric, stencils or découpage.

Magic shelves

Although they cannot take anything heavy, these great-looking shelves are ideal for lamps and ornaments. For safety's sake they are best kept to a maximum length of about 30cm (12in), but several can be grouped together to make a chic wall display, ideal for unusual objects.

EQUIPMENT

MATERIALS AND

Tape measure

Pencil

2.5 x 2.5cm (1 x 1in) timber batten: long enough for each shelf

Handsaw or jigsaw with timber-cutting blade

Drill with 6mm masonry bit; 3mm wood bit for pilot holes

Spirit level

Bradawl

6mm wall plugs (solid or cavity)

Woodscrews: 4.5cm (1¾in) size 10; 7.5cm (3in) size 8

Screwdriver; or screwdriver bit for drill

20 x 7.5cm (8 x 3in) new or scrap timber: allow 30cm (12in) maximum per shelf

Router with rebate-cutter bit (optional)

Wood glue

1 Measure and cut timber battens the same length as your intended shelves with the handsaw or jigsaw. Drill two screw holes through each batten using the 3mm wood bit and position them on the wall using a spirit level to get them straight. Use the screw holes to mark drilling points on the wall with the bradawl, then drill holes into the wall with the 6mm masonry bit, put in the wall plugs and screw the battens to the wall using 4.5cm (1¾in) screws.

2 Cut small lengths of shelf – maximum 30cm (12in) – from the 20 x 7.5cm (8 x 3in) timber. Then use either a handsaw or a router to create a 2.5 x 2.5cm (1 x 1in) rebate all along the length of one edge. The longer the shelf, the more invaluable a router will be for this task. Once the wood is held firmly in place and the sliding guide on the router is set to 2.5cm (1in), simply run the tool along the edge of the timber to make a perfect rebate.

3 Glue a shelf on to each batten so that the batten sits snugly in the rebate, then screw down through the top back edge, close to the wall, with 7.5cm (3in) screws, ensuring that the screws finish flush with the surface of the shelf.

TOP TIP

These shelves can be left raw and rustic if you wish. Alternatively, sand them down and experiment with varnish, wood stain, paint or metallic spray. You could even decorate the edges with fabric or paper cut-outs.

Etched cupboard doors

An open shelf unit in a living room is highly practical for storage but you may not want everything on view all the time, especially if the shelves become a bit cluttered. Anna's perspex doors are opaque enough to mask the paraphernalia behind, but translucent enough to keep a feeling of light and space. They are also an effective way of giving a tired piece of furniture a brand new look without having to run to tremendous expense.

1 Use the screwdriver to unhinge existing cupboard doors and then measure them, or measure the length and width of the area where you wish to add doors. If your Perspex is not ready-cut, cut it to size with the jigsaw. Sand the edges of the Perspex then wipe carefully to ensure it is absolutely clean. If working freehand, use the Chinagraph pencil to draw the leaf shape on to the Perspex, then turn the sheet over to see the leaf shape through the Perspex. If using a template, place the drawing under the Perspex and trace around it with the Chinagraph pencil. Paint the shape of the leaf with masking fluid and an artist's brush, taking care not to slip outside the outline. As the fluid dries it will become quite rubbery.

2 Once the fluid is dry, cover the whole surface of the Perspex with glass-etch spray. This should be applied in short blasts to create lots of thin even layers and avoid a patchy finish. When satisfied with the coverage, leave the Perspex to dry for at least half an hour at normal room temperature.

3 Once the glass-etch is dry use a small pointed knife or scalpel to lift a corner of the masking fluid, then pull it off like elastic bands. It will have shielded the leaf motif from the glass-etch spray and left the shape clearly visible.

4 Finally, add the hinges to the doors. Work out their positions, predrill the Perspex to prevent it splitting and use small bolts to attach them. Two hinges per door should be adequate for a cabinet but a larger cupboard may need an extra hinge placed midway between the other two. Attach magnetic fasteners to the cabinet and doors using adhesive.

TOP TIP
Genuine etched glass is both expensive and heavy so this technique makes achieving a contemporary look cheaper and much simpler to do. Always go for a large-scale motif like the leaf, rather than something small and fiddly that lacks impact.

Japanese-style seating

Homes have to be flexible to accommodate changing needs and extra seating will never be wasted, particularly when you are entertaining. Graham's simple, stylish idea, with an oriental twist, consists of two separate parts placed together to become a single unit. The seating can be assembled and dismantled extremely easily and is quick and inexpensive to make.

1 Put the long sides of each pair of breeze blocks side by side and bond together with cement: mix the cement with water in the bucket, using a trowel. Leave the blocks to dry. Sand the wooden slats and brush on a coat of white emulsion diluted 50:50 with water, then wipe off the paint to create a 'limed' effect. When dry, seal with acrylic varnish and leave to dry again. Butt the slats side by side on a workbench. Cut two strips of timber batten slightly shorter than the depth of the seat with the saw, and position them at each end of the slats. Ensure that the distance between the battens is slightly shorter than that between the breeze blocks, so that when the seat is in position the battens do not clash with the blocks. Drill two holes through each batten and part of the way through the slats. Screw the battens to the slats and turn the seat over.

2 Place the foam seat pads on the bench. Sit down and mark the height of the backrest cushions. Fix the saddle clips 15cm (6in) above this marked height at either end of the seat. Measure the distance between the clips, add on 10cm (4in) and cut the dowelling to this length. Paint the pole black, allow it to dry and then varnish.

3 Cut four 25 x 7.5cm (10 x 3in) rectangles from the black canvas, hem the edges and join the ends to form loops. Sew the loops on to the headrests, then slide the loops on to the pole and fit the pole on to the wall with the saddle clips.

EQUIPMENT

MATERIALS AND

Four breeze blocks
Packet of quick-drying cement
Water
Bucket
Trowel
Sandpaper
10 x 5cm (4 x 2in) timber slats
Emulsion paint: white
Emulsion brush
Acrylic varnish
5cm (2in) paintbrush
Tape measure
Pencil
5 x 2.5cm (2 x 1in) timber batten
Saw
Drill
Size 8 woodscrews
Screwdriver
Two black-covered foam seat pads
Two black-covered foam backrest cushions
Two saddle clips
5cm (2in) wooden dowelling: the length of the seat
Eggshell or gloss paint: black
1m (3ft) black canvas fabric
Scissors
Sewing machine or needle and thread

1

2

3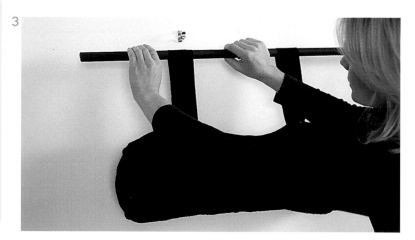

Slatted radiator cabinet

Even brand-new radiators can be something of an eyesore, but in the absence of a better alternative a good-looking cabinet could solve the problem. This one, designed by Graham, has cut-out slats that allow the air to circulate freely, making it a practical as well as an attractive option. With its muslin backing, it has a futuristic feel that is perfect for an ultramodern setting.

MATERIALS AND EQUIPMENT

Tape measure

Pencil

Sheet of 12mm (½in) MDF

Jigsaw with timber-cutting blade

Sandpaper

1 x 6.25cm (½ x 2½in) timber slats: About 8, depending on the size of the radiator

Drill

Countersink

Wood glue

Size 8 woodscrews and screwdriver

Filler

Profile gauge (a tool that is pressed against awkward shapes to copy their outline)

Primer

Paint

7.5cm (3in) paintbrush

Staple gun

Muslin fabric: to cover radiator front with 5cm (2in) turning all around

Scissors

1 Measure the height, depth and width of the radiator, adding 10cm (4in) to the height and width for a generous fit and to allow air to circulate. The top of the cabinet should overhang both the sides and the front of the radiator. Mark out the side and top pieces on the MDF and cut them out with the jigsaw. Sand all the cut edges. The timber slats and muslin will form the front of the cabinet.

2 Start to assemble the cabinet. Mark where the front slats will meet the side panels and countersink holes through the side panels and into the slats at each of these points. Spread a line of wood glue along the

1

2

edge of one side piece and carefully push the slats into place. Repeat on the other side, then drive in the side-panel screws to hold the slats firmly.

3 Fit the top with all the back edges aligned so that it overlaps slightly at the sides and the front. Fill all the screw holes with filler, allow to dry and then sand smooth.

4 If you have a skirting board, use a profile gauge to fit the cabinet neatly over it. Mark the profile on the back edge of the side panels, then cut out with a jigsaw, and sand. Prime and paint the cabinet.

5 Finally, when the paint is dry, lay the cabinet on the floor and turn it over. Spread the muslin out over the back of the slatted area and use a staple gun to attach it to the inside of the frame, keeping the fabric taut as you move around. Cut away any excess fabric and position the cabinet over the radiator.

TOP TIP
The basic frame of this cabinet could easily be adapted to suit other styles. Chicken wire, for example, could be used instead of muslin for an industrial edge.

3

4

5

Star cupboard doors

This is a quick and clever idea for a simple cupboard that can fit into any size of alcove. Shelves above a curtain rail fixed behind the doors will convert it into a complete wardrobe. The cut-out motif can be as simple or as complicated as you like.

1 Measure the height and width of the alcove and cut corresponding lengths of timber batten with the jigsaw. Secure the battens down the sides and along the floor and ceiling of the alcove. Those at the top and bottom will act as backstops for the doors when they are closed. Mark pilot holes in the walls with the bradawl or using the drill and the 3mm wood bit. Then drill holes into the walls with the 6mm masonry bit, put in the wall plugs and screw the battens to the walls using the 4.5cm (1½in) screws. If the floor is wood it will only need screws.

2 Measure the height and width of the alcove and then cut a pair of doors to fit from the MDF or plywood. Make a paper template of a star, or your chosen motif. Mark the position for the cut-out in exactly the same spot on each door and then trace around the template. Make a hole in the motif using the 10mm drill bit, then insert the jigsaw blade and cut out the shape. If you are particularly careful, you may be able to use the cut-out pieces to make the handles for your cupboard (see Steps 4 and 5)

3 Hang the doors using two concealed adjustable hinges on each door. They should be positioned about 50cm (20in) from the top and bottom of the doors. Adjust the hinges to make sure the doors hang straight and level.

TOP TIP

If you have a simple motif like a flower in the fabric or wallpaper of your room, you can adapt this as the cut-out motif. Moons or rockets would look brilliant on a child's cupboard and might encourage them to tidy up!

4 Use the paper template again to mark out two more shapes on some spare pieces of timber (see Step 2). These are going to form the handles of the doors.

5 Place a small square of timber behind each shape to hold the handle away from the door and allow some grip. Mark the position for the handles and secure everything in place with glue and 5cm (2in) screws. Fix the handles from the back so that no screw heads show on the front.

EQUIPMENT

MATERIALS AND

Tape measure

Pencil

5 x 2.5cm (2 x 1in) timber batten: to go around the top, bottom and sides of the alcove

Jigsaw with timber-cutting blade

Bradawl

Drill with 6mm masonry bit; 3mm wood bit for pilot holes; 10mm wood drill bit

6mm wall plugs (solid or cavity)

Woodscrews: 4.5cm (1¾in) size 8; 5cm (2in) size 8

Screwdriver; or screwdriver drill bit

2cm (¾in) MDF or plywood: about two 2.4 x 1.2m (8 x 4ft) sheets

Paper for template

Four concealed adjustable hinges

Wood glue

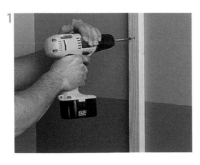

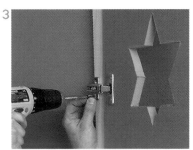

3

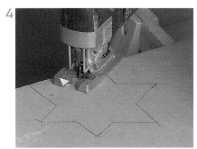

4

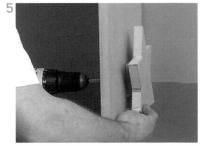

5

Ornate chair backs

Surprising revamps of cupboards and flooring are no longer such a novelty, but dull, functional chairs can also be given a fresh face. This project depends on a jigsaw, so your skill in using it will determine how spectacular a transformation you can achieve.

1 Cut the seat back out of an old wooden chair with the handsaw, leaving the uprights intact.

2 Measure the remaining gap and decide on the height of the new back. Use a paper template to mark out your design on 2.5cm (1in) MDF so that it fits in the gap and cut it out with the jigsaw. Make sure the design allows for the MDF to be attached to the uprights in at least two places on each side.

3 Fix the new back to the existing uprights at the points where the two meet, using wood glue and screws. Drill pilot holes for the screws and ensure that the screw heads lie flush with the surface of the uprights. Sand down any rough edges and then paint the chair.

TOP TIP

Once you've finished making the backs to your chairs, turn them into dramatic thrones by finishing them with gold or silver paint.

EQUIPMENT

MATERIALS AND

Handsaw

Tape measure

Pencil

Paper for template

2.5cm (1in) MDF or plywood: about 60 x 90cm (2 x 3ft) per chair

Jigsaw with scroll-cutting blade

Wood glue

Drill with 3mm wood bit for pilot holes

4cm (1½in) size 8 woodscrews

Screwdriver; or screwdriver bit for drill

Sandpaper

Paint

1

2

3
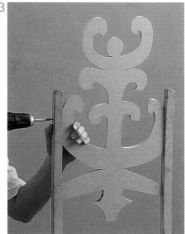

The weekend wardrobe

Wardrobes can be expensive to buy and a headache when it comes to moving them. Laurence's simple construction will store clothes and shoes conveniently and is built into the corner of a bedroom. It also has the added advantage of being quick and easy to assemble. To give your finished wardrobe a really smart finish, don't forget to paint the insides of the doors as well as the outside. Before you start, be sure to check you have enough clearance to open the doors.

1 Measure and mark lines across the floor and ceiling in a corner of the room to make two identical rectangles the size of your intended wardrobe. Cut timber battens to match the lengths of these lines with a handsaw or jigsaw. Secure the battens to the floor and ceiling. For the ceiling, mark pilot holes with the bradawl or using the drill and the 3mm wood bit. Then drill holes into the ceiling with the 6mm masonry bit, put in the wall plugs and screw the battens to the ceiling. A wood floor will only need screws. The corners where the battens meet can be either mitred or butt-joined as they will not be visible once the wardrobe is built. Fix further battens with wall plugs and screws up each wall, as described above, to link up with the ends of the floor and ceiling battens, creating the wardrobe frame.

2 Measure and cut two wardrobe doors and one side panel from the MDF and hold them in place to check they fit correctly. Drill pilot holes around three sides of the side panel, one about every 30cm (12in), and use these to attach the MDF to the floor, wall and ceiling battens with glue and screws. Ensure the screws are driven in far enough so that the heads are flush with the surface of the MDF.

3 Use the hole-cutter bit to make two holes down the long outside edge of each door where the hinges are to be fitted. The hinges should be placed about 30cm (12in) from the top and bottom of the door.

4 Push one hinge into each of the four mounting holes and secure tightly in place with the specialist screws supplied.

5 Use a chisel to prop the doors clear of the floor while you mark and then screw the hinges to the walls of the wardrobe. Once secure, you can adjust the hinges to make sure the doors open and close with ease.

6 Finally, use up offcuts of MDF to make door handles. Two 15cm (6in) squares with a smaller square behind each can be glued and screwed in from the back at a convenient height. Be sure the screws are not so long that the points come through on to the fronts of the handles. Alternatively, take a trip to a DIY store. Most stock a huge range of ready-made handles for you to choose from.

Tape measure

Pencil

5 x 2.5cm (2 x 1in) timber batten: about 9m (30ft)

Handsaw or jigsaw with timber-cutting blade

Bradawl

Drill with 6mm masonry bit; 3mm wood bit for pilot holes; hole-cutter bit (usually on display with hinges in DIY stores)

6mm wall plugs (solid or cavity)

4.5cm (1¾in) size 8 woodscrews

Screwdriver; or screwdriver bit for drill

2cm (¾in) MDF or plywood: two 2.4 x 1.2m (8 x 4ft) sheets should be sufficient

Wood glue

Four concealed adjustable hinges

Chisel

TOP TIP

Once constructed, your wardrobe can be decorated as you choose. If you opt for a dark shade for the outside, it's a good idea to paint the inside a lighter colour. You'll be surprised at how much easier it will be to see your clothes and shoes.

4
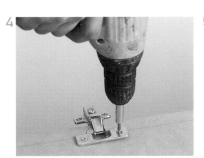

5

6

Copper tubing insert table

Transforming an item of furniture by introducing a new material into its structure is an inexpensive way to alter the feel of a room. In this project Linda has revitalized a table with a copper tubing insert, which looks sensational and gives a heat-resistant surface.

1 Decide on the dimensions of the new table-top, and draw the shape on to the sheet of MDF (use a plate as a guide when drawing rounded corners). Using a jigsaw, cut out the shape and sand the edges smooth.

2 In the centre of the table-top mark out a lengthways rectangle wide enough to lay five copper tubes side by side. Use a router to gouge out this channel to a depth of 18mm, (⅝in) then sand smooth.

3 Paint the table-top with at least two coats of emulsion and leave to dry. Using the pipe cutter, cut the copper piping into lengths to fit the channel and smooth the edges with sandpaper. Spread silicone sealant into the channel, then bed each length of piping into it and leave to dry.

4 Spray the whole table-top with at least two coats of varnish. When dry, secure the top to an old table or table legs with long woodscrews. Turn the table upside down and paint the base with eggshell or emulsion topped with varnish, as for the table-top. Finally, for a stylish finishing touch, paint the edges of the table with copper paint.

EQUIPMENT

MATERIALS AND

Tape measure
Pencil
Sheet of 2.5cm (1in) MDF
Plate or saucer
Jigsaw with timber-cutting blade
Sandpaper
Router
Emulsion paint: for table-top
5cm (2in) paintbrush
Pipe cutter
15mm diameter copper tubing
Clear silicone sealant
Spray polyurethane varnish
Old table or table legs
Long woodscrews
Screwdriver
Eggshell or emulsion paint: to match table-top
Copper paint (optional)

Découpage cabinet

Far Eastern influences have a lasting appeal and these days it is easy to buy all kinds of Chinese accessories. Linda used oriental newsprint to give this cabinet a new lease of life. As well as being inexpensive, its intriguing graphic script with flashes of scarlet makes it an ideal material for découpage. The golden circle on the front added an extra touch of sophistication and enhanced the oriental effect.

EQUIPMENT

MATERIALS AND

Old cupboard or chest of drawers, sanded and/or cleaned

Chinese newspapers

Scissors

PVA glue

5cm (2in) paintbrush

Acrylic varnish

Sheet of copper foil

Circular template, e.g. dinner plate

Pencil

Blunt scissors

Magnetic fasteners

Screws

Screwdriver

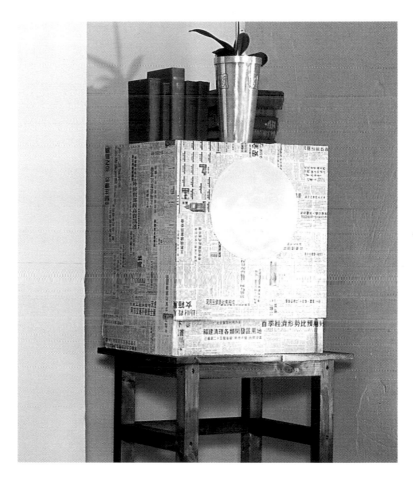

1 Cut the newspapers into sheets, taking out any unwanted script or pictures. Spread some strips on the furniture and brush with PVA glue, working outwards from the centre to avoid trapping air bubbles. The glue will soak through the paper and make it stick. Brush the top sheet of paper with a little more glue to get a smooth surface. Continue until the whole unit is covered and leave to dry.

2 Protect and seal the paper surface of the unit with at least two coats of acrylic varnish.

3 If the unit has doors, these can be embellished with a circle of thin copper foil. Draw a circle on the foil using a dinner plate or similar as a template, then cut it out and cut through the centre to make two semicircles. (Use blunt scissors to cut the foil, as it will damage sharp ones for good.) Stick the two halves to the unit with PVA glue. Finally, measure the position for the magnetic fasteners and screw them into place.

False-depth alcove shelves

Linda's simple chunky-looking MDF shelves are not even fixed to the wall, but simply rest on battens. They look much more expensive than they are, and the illusion of depth is created by a strip of MDF secured along the front edge. This strip also makes the shelves sturdy enough for heavier items like books.

1 Use the spirit level to help measure and mark out positions for the battens that will support each shelf. Cut the battens with a handsaw or jigsaw to 2.5cm (1in) less than the depth of the finished shelves or angle the ends so that they will not interfere with the facing strips to be fitted to the front edges. Mark pilot holes in the walls on either side of the alcove with the bradawl or using the drill and the 3mm wood bit. Then drill holes into the walls with the 6mm masonry bit, put in the wall plugs and screw the battens to the walls. The battens must be horizontal both left to right and front to back, otherwise the shelves will not sit straight.

2 Measure and cut the shelves from MDF. Remember that the alcove may not be square all the way up. Use a sliding bevel to cut a shelf for each position. A sliding bevel can be locked off at any angle and that setting used to transfer the measurement to the material you are cutting to fit.

3 Cut 7.5cm (3in) strips of MDF to the same width as each shelf, then attach them to the front edges of each shelf with glue and screws.

4 Once complete, the shelves simply rest in place on top of the battens. Assuming they are straight they will not require securing in place and can easily be lifted out for painting.

1

2
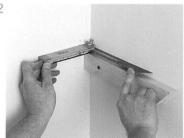

3
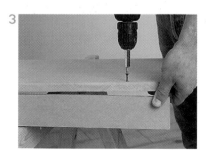

4

Punched metal doors

If you are thinking of revamping some tired old cupboard doors, Linda's idea is a really exciting and effective technique to try. It's not a quick project so be prepared to put in some time and effort, but the results will more than justify your hard work. If you are worried about tackling something more complex, try and choose a simple design and plan it out carefully in advance, it will save you time and materials in the end. Do take care when handling sheets of zinc as edges can be sharp.

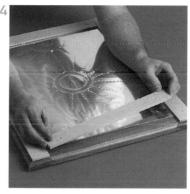

1 Remove the existing cupboard doors with a screwdriver and lay them on a flat surface. Measure the front of them and cut matching zinc panels 2.5cm (1in) smaller all around. Use tin snips to cut the zinc carefully.

2 Measure 5cm (2in) strips of 5mm (¼in) MDF to fit all around the outer edges of the zinc panels and cut with a handsaw or jigsaw. You can mitre or flat-join these strips, depending on your time frame. Flat-joining is quicker. Turn over all the MDF strips, marking each one so that you can replace it exactly, and use a ruler and pencil to mark a 2.5cm (1in) rebate on what will become the inside edge of the rear face. Use a plane to slice out a shallow rebate, just deep enough to hold the zinc panel.

3 Make a paper template for your design and then use the felt-tip pen to mark it on to the zinc panels. Use a large nail and hammer to punch out the design. Keep the design simple if you have limited time, as each panel has to match the first and the punching stage can be quite time consuming.

4 Place the punched panel in the centre of the door and secure it in place by fixing the MDF strips around it with wood glue and screws. The edges of the zinc should sit neatly in the shallow rebates in the MDF strips. Any holes can then be filled, and the doors sanded with fine-grade sandpaper and painted with emulsion if required, before being rehung.

TOP TIP

The pattern shown here was inspired by a Mexican theme, but you can use any motif you choose. Browse through books and magazines for ideas. A foolproof way to transfer a design on to the zinc is to photocopy the outline, enlarge it to the size you want and tape it on to the zinc. You can then simply punch the zinc through the paper following the design.

French farmhouse wardrobe

This project will save you the expense of a new wardrobe by updating a tired-looking old one. Graham used a distressed paint effect and blue-and-white gingham panels to lend a country flavour, but your own choice of fabric and finish will determine the style. New handles will complete the transformation from shabby to stylish.

1 Take the doors off your wardrobe with a screwdriver and carefully mark a line about 5cm (2in) in from the existing mouldings. Use a jigsaw to cut out the resulting shape from each panel. To start the cut, drill a pilot hole with the 10mm wood bit in the unwanted part of each panel to insert the jigsaw blade. (Alternatively, if your wardrobe is beyond saving, you can buy replacement doors from a DIY store.)

2 Sand the inner edges of the new holes to make them smooth.

3 Using a pair of pliers or tin snips, cut out pieces of chicken wire about 2.5cm (1in) wider all round than the holes in the door panels (see Top Tip). Working on the inside of the door, pin or staple a piece of chicken wire to the back of each hole, ensuring the wire is taut across the hole. Cut panels of fabric to fit behind the wire. The fabric can either lie flat, or be gathered, so allow enough for your choice, plus a hem of about 5cm (2in) all around. Stitch or glue the hem, then pin or staple the panels, or glue them with fabric glue, to hang behind the wire. Rehang the doors.

4 Cut three lengths of architrave to correspond to the front and two sides of the wardrobe. Mitre the ends for a snug join, using the mitre block, and fix the architrave to the top of the wardrobe with wood glue. Hammer in several panel pins to secure it firmly in place. Use a nail punch to make sure the panel pins are pushed down into the architrave. If there is room, you can fit architrave to the bottom edge too. Finish off the revamped wardrobe with a light sanding and a coat of acrylic primer before applying your emulsion colour and a sealing layer of acrylic varnish.

Screwdriver; or screwdriver bit for drill

Tape measure

Pencil

Drill with 10mm wood bit

Jigsaw with timber-cutting blade

Sandpaper

Pliers or tin snips

Chicken wire: to cover each door

2.5cm (1in) panel pins and hammer; or staple gun and staples; or U-shaped staples to be hammered in

Fabric: to cover each door, extra if you want to gather it

Fabric glue (optional)

5cm (2in) architrave: to go around top and possibly bottom of wardrobe

Mitre block

Wood glue

Nail punch

TOP TIP

Chicken wire has extremely sharp ends that will catch on clothes in the wardrobe. To prevent this, bend the edges of the chicken wire under before you fasten it down. Sheer muslin behind the wire will add a cool, contemporary look. Alternatively, a plain, bright fabric can create a flash of a breath-takingly bold, contrasting colour that won't dominate the room.

Tongue-and-groove table-top

Flexible furniture is in demand these days and here is a brilliant way to expand your dining table temporarily for those big occasions. You can also conceal a scruffy old table beneath a smart top, but do check that the table legs are strong and sound enough to take the extra weight and wear.

MATERIALS AND EQUIPMENT

Tape measure

Pencil

10cm (4in) or 15cm (6in) tongue-and-groove floorboards: to cover the old table-top with a 10cm (4in) overlap all around

Handsaw or jigsaw with timber-cutting blade

Wood glue

2 sash clamps (optional)

5 x 2.5cm (2 x 1in) timber batten: twice the length and twice the width of the old table-top

Drill with 3mm wood bit for pilot holes

4cm (1½in) size 8 woodscrews

Screwdriver; or screwdriver bit for drill

Paint, varnish or Danish Oil

1 Measure the old table-top and add 10cm (4in) extra on all sides. Cut enough tongue-and-groove planks of equal length to cover the total area using a handsaw or jigsaw. Use wood glue to glue the planks side by side. Sash clamps would be very helpful to hold everything rigid until the glue dries.

2 Once it's dry and firm, place the new table-top face down and lie the old table on top, exactly in the middle. Draw a pencil line around the old table and then remove it.

3 Cut four timber battens to form a frame around the outline you have just drawn. Attach them to the underside of the new top with glue and screws. The corners can be simply butt-joined. Make sure the screws are not longer than the combined depth of the battens and the top, otherwise they may come through on to the table-top. The border will not only hold the tongue-and-groove planks together, but it will also fit snugly over the old top and stop any movement.

4 Turn everything the right way up and lower the new top into place. Sand any rough edges. The table-top can now be painted or varnished. If you prefer a natural timber finish, protect the top from food and drink stains with a coat of Danish Oil.

TOP TIP

If you only need the extra table room for infrequent entertaining, you can reclaim your space afterwards by lifting off the top and storing it under a bed or in a garage when it's not in use.

Block shelving

A visit to a builder's merchant can inspire you with a whole range of interesting materials, especially if you are after an industrial edge to your home. If your living room is not in keeping with this look, consider using it to bring real style to a bathroom.

1 Place two brick starter grids on the wall about 90cm (3ft) apart, use a spirit level to check they are aligned and secure them in place with the fixings supplied. Loose-stack concrete or thermolite blocks to calculate the height of the unit and the number of shelves. Two blocks between shelves will make a balanced-looking unit and the shelves can go up to the ceiling if you wish. Once the blocks are arranged, mix up the mortar and start laying the blocks in place with the trowel.

2 The brick starter grids have tabs that fold down across each block, tying the whole construction firmly to the wall. Use a pair of pliers to prise the tabs down over the blocks. Measure the distance between the outer edges of each stack of blocks and add 10cm (4in) to each end to give the length of the shelves. Measure from the front edge of the blocks to the wall and add on 1.25cm (½in) for the width of the shelves. Cut the required number of shelves from MDF using a handsaw or jigsaw.

3 When the blocks are two deep (or your chosen depth) on either side, put a final layer of mortar on each brick. Hammer the panel pins part way through the MDF shelves where you want to fix them to the bricks, then lay the shelves on to the wet mortar. Finish hammering the pins through the MDF into the mortar. As you place each shelf on the mortar check with a spirit level that it is level. Then, put a small amount of mortar on the top of each shelf-end to hold the next supporting blocks in place. Repeat the process until the stack is as high as you want.

4 Leave the mortar to dry overnight and then cut narrow strips of MDF, 5cm (2in) wide and the length and depth of the shelves. Glue and pin them along the front and sides of each shelf. Finally, paint the shelves for a professional finish.

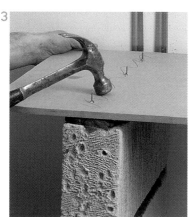

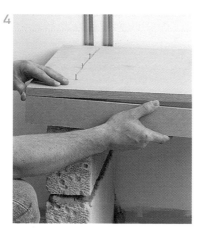

EQUIPMENT

MATERIALS AND

Two brick starter grids with fixing nails

Tape measure and pencil

Spirit level with timber straightedge

Concrete or thermolite blocks painted the colour of your choice

Mortar mix and trowel

Pliers

1.25cm (½in) MDF or plywood: about two 2.4 x 1.2m (8 x 4ft) sheets

Handsaw or jigsaw with timber-cutting blade

2.5cm (1in) panel pins

Hammer

Wood glue

Paint (the same colour as that used on the concrete blocks)

TOP TIP

These shelves would also be practical and inexpensive for storage in a garage, tool shed or cellar.

Silver detailing on furniture

Linda used metallic leaf to perk up this chest of drawers and give it a contemporary touch. Silver may not be the first colour that springs to mind for furniture decoration, but it looks wonderful especially when used with pale blues, greys and lilacs.

1 Prepare the chest of drawers by unscrewing the handles and then cleaning and sanding it. Apply a coat of white wood primer so that it's ready to be painted. When dry, draw a circle on the front of the chest, making sure it is centrally positioned. To do this, find the centre point (by drawing faint lines dividing the front in half from top to bottom and from left to right to find where they cross). Tap a nail into the centre point and tie a piece of string to it. Tie a pencil to the other end of the string, making sure that when the string is taut the circle will be of the right diameter.

2 Apply two coats of your emulsion colour, excluding the area inside the circle.

3 When this base colour is dry, mask off the circle by sticking a treble row of low-tack masking tape around it. The strips of tape should be about 5cm (2in) long. Apply spray adhesive all over the circle. Once this is tacky, apply aluminium leaf from transfer paper. This comes as squares and is fairly easy to apply, but work on one small area at a time and allow for overlaps. If you do end up with any gaps, just spray on some more adhesive and patch them with aluminium leaf. Once the circle is covered, allow it to set for an hour. Brush off the excess leaf with a soft paintbrush, peel off the tape and give the whole piece of furniture a coat of clear gloss varnish. Re-attach or replace the handles.

EQUIPMENT

MATERIALS AND

- Small screwdriver
- Sandpaper
- White wood primer
- Pencil
- Nail
- String
- Emulsion paint
- Low-tack masking tape
- Spray adhesive (e.g. Multi Mount from 3M)
- Aluminium leaf
- Soft paintbrush
- Clear gloss varnish

TOP TIP
Use gold leaf instead of silver for dramatic results on cream-painted furniture.

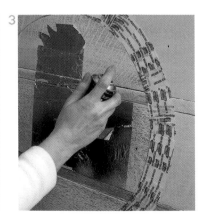

Multitoned filing cabinet

Working from home is becoming increasingly common, but not everyone has a dedicated office space. If you combine work and relaxation in the same space, Graham's design will help to make your metal filing cabinets a little less functional and more friendly so that you can truly forget about work after hours. Here, Graham used a shading technique on a cabinet with a number of drawers of varying sizes, but the effect would work just as well on a more conventional filing cabinet.

1 Remove any flaking paint or rust with a wire brush and then sand the cabinet well all over by hand, or with a power sander, for a good 'key' (roughness) that will help the paint to adhere. Work quickly with the coarse sandpaper to remove heavy wear and tear, then follow with the medium paper. Finally, use the fine paper for a smooth finish.

2 Wipe the cabinet down to remove dust. If you want to protect the handles from paint, wrap them in masking tape. Brush or spray on the metal primer and allow to dry thoroughly.

3 Work out how many gradations of top colour you want and mark on the drawers with a pencil where they should fall. If the drawers are deep, you may want to have two or more gradations on each one. To make the gradation more effective, blend colours slightly where they meet

so that there is no definite 'join'. Spray or brush on the top coat starting at the bottom with the darkest colour and working upwards to finish with the palest shade. Spray the cabinet with a coat of polyurethane varnish to protect it from wear and tear.

EQUIPMENT

MATERIALS AND

- Metal filing cabinet
- Wire brush
- Coarse-, medium- and fine-grade sandpaper for metal surfaces; or a power sander
- Masking tape (optional)
- Metal primer
- Pencil
- Enamel paints for metal surfaces: from pale to dark tones, e.g. palest lilac to deepest purple
- 5cm (2in) paintbrushes
- Polyurethane varnish

TOP TIP

If you cannot find the right
gradation of colour in ready-
mixed shades, or want to use
a large number of different
tones, the best approach is
to buy satin or gloss paint in,
for example, dark purple and
white only, so that you can
then mix your own shades.
This technique is not limited
to the office, but can look
really effective on a bedside
table or chest of drawers.

Accessories

The all-important finishing touches to any room are the accessories, which can bring a completely fresh look, changing the atmosphere from winter to summer or from day to evening. Sometimes they can simply cheer up a tired-looking room. If you've never made anything before, you can build your confidence by starting with accessories.

Sunburst mirror

The retro trend shows no sign of abating, and Linda's sunburst mirror has just the right look. The starburst effect is really easy to reproduce with lengths of dowelling and copper spray. This project will also save you quite a bit on the price of these types of mirrors in the shops.

1 Place the mirror on to the MDF sheet and draw around it with the pencil. Then draw another circle outside this one, about 10cm (4in) bigger all the way around, that is, 20cm (8in) larger in diameter than the inner circle. Cut around the outer circle with the jigsaw. Attach the mirror to the centre of the MDF circle with panel adhesive.

2 Cut the dowelling to a variety of different lengths, but none less than 10cm (4in) long or they will not overlap the MDF mount. The longer you make the longest rods, and the greater the range of lengths you include, the more dramatic a 'sunburst' effect you will create. Sand each rod to remove sharp edges. Spread panel adhesive on to the MDF border around the mirror in sections of about 10cm (4in) at a time. Press lengths of dowelling on to the glue, positioning them so that at the edge of the glass the tips meet one another all the way around with no gaps, before fanning

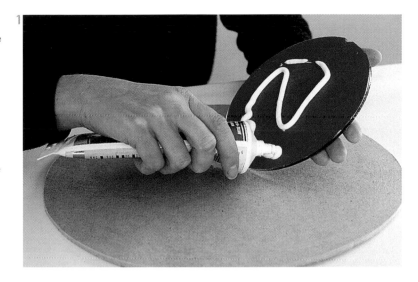

out to make the sunburst shape. Work all the way around in sections until complete, then allow to dry overnight.

3 When the adhesive is dry, protect the outer edges of the mirror with masking tape and then spray thoroughly to cover all the dowelling and the MDF mount with copper spray paint. No wood should be visible. Hang the mirror using a picture-hanging kit.

TOP TIP
A mirror like this is an excellent way to add interest on a blank expanse of wall. As you can make it as large as you wish, it is ideal for a characterless space, such as a dark hallway, or dull corridor, that needs some kind of interest or focal point. You can enhance its impact even further by positioning lighting to maximize the shadows and reflections it casts on the walls.

EQUIPMENT

MATERIALS AND

Circular mirror with polished edges
Sheet of 12mm (½in) MDF sheet
Pencil
Round template
Jigsaw with timber-cutting blade
Panel adhesive
Dowelling in a variety of diameters between 3mm (⅛in) and 9mm (½in)
Saw
Sandpaper
Masking tape
Copper spray paint
Picture-hanging kit

Slip-on chair covers

Linda's slip-on chair covers are the perfect answer to shabby dining chairs. You might not want to use them on a daily basis but they will certainly pep up a room for a special celebration, and you'll feel as though you own two different sets of chairs! If you're feeling inspired, why not make a second set of covers using a different style or shade of fabric, then you'll have even more opportunity to ring the changes.

1 Make a template for the cover by draping newspaper over the chair and cutting individual pieces to fit each plane. Add a 2cm (⅝in) seam allowance to each pattern piece. Pin them all together on the chair so that you know you have a good fit. Number and name all the paper pieces (1 seat, 2 backrest, 3 back, 4 front, 5 and 6 sides) with the pencil and unpin them.

2 Pin the pattern pieces on to the linen and cut out. Remove the pins and paper and copy the number on to each piece of fabric with tailor's chalk. Sew together, and keep placing the cover over the chair to ensure the correct fit. When completed, slip the cover over the chair and pin up and sew the hem. Press the seams flat with a hot iron. Measure the chair width and the height from the top of the back almost down to floor level. Add a 2cm (⅝in) seam allowance all around and cut the raw silk banner to these measurements. To prevent fraying, fold the edges of the silk over twice, then pin and stitch all around. Press flat with a warm iron.

3 Lay the banner on a flat work-surface and with a pencil draw a random pattern of circles on it, using a saucer as a template. Mark the centre of each circle. Squeeze a small blob of fabric paint on to the centre point so that it sits raised on the surface, then continue squeezing blobs out in a spiral from the centre to the edge of the circle. Repeat for the other circles. Dry the paint with the slow speed of the hairdryer. When dry, hand-stitch the banner neatly to the top seam of the chair cover.

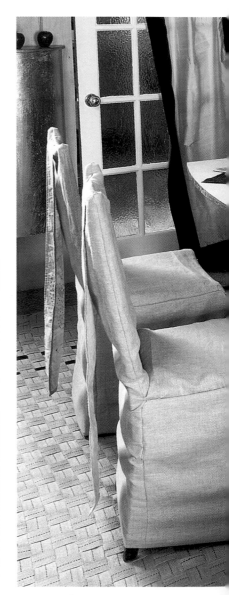

EQUIPMENT

MATERIALS AND

Dining chair with high, simply shaped back and no arms

Newspaper

Scissors

Pins

Pencil

Approximately 1m (3ft) linen fabric for each chair cover

Tailor's chalk

Sewing machine with appropriate thread

Iron

Raw silk

Saucer

Fabric paint (3-D)

Hairdryer

Needle and thread

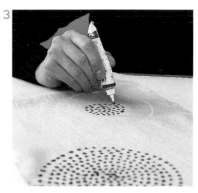

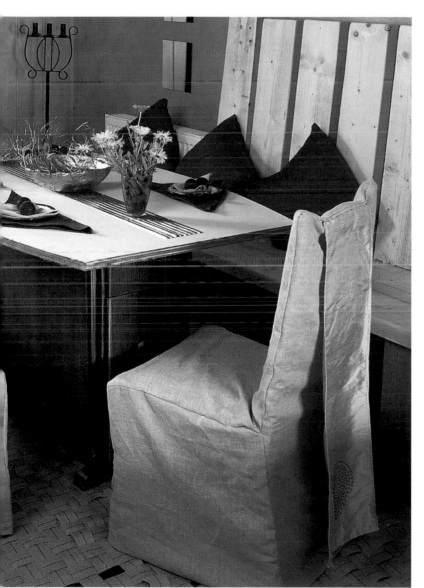

TOP TIP

Contrast is an important facet of successful design. Here, the silk banner provides a smooth, sheeny surface against grainy linen, and can also be used to echo the colour and detail of the curtains or another key feature. The knobbly finish of the painted swirls adds another twist.

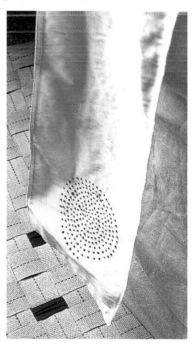

Bathmat cushions

Cushions are a staple of decorating, but they do not have to be predictable. Linda's bathmat covers inject quirky humour into a room and add an element of surprise. They also have tremendous textural impact. Keep your eyes and your mind open for other materials that can be used in unexpected situations.

1 Dye the bathmats with the fabric dye, following the instructions on the pack, and leave to dry thoroughly. You can use absolutely any shade you wish.

2 For each cushion, measure the cushion pad and add 3cm (1¼in) all around. Cut a bathmat to this size and then cut a canvas piece of the same size. The canvas will make the back of the cushion.

3 Pin a panel of bathmat to the canvas piece, right sides together, and sew along three sides. Turn right-side out and insert the cushion pad. Tuck in the raw edges along the open side and sew together.

EQUIPMENT

MATERIALS AND

White bathmats
Fabric dye
Salt, for use with dye
Tape measure
Cushion pads
Scissors
Cotton canvas backing fabric
Pins
Needle and thread

Gauze banner

Anna's beautiful banner demonstrates the contemporary theme of mixing textures. It can be used to conceal a storage unit or as a window treatment.

1 Measure the area you want to cover and then add 6cm (2½in) to the width and 13cm (5¼in) to the length. Cut the canvas to these measurements. Pin up a 3cm (1¼in) hem on three sides and make a 10cm (4in) hem along the top edge to act as a channel for the curtain wire from which the banner will hang. Neatly sew and then press all the hems.

2 Measure the finished canvas panel, deduct 10cm (4in) all round and cut a piece of organza to these measurements. On all four sides roll under the raw edges by about 1cm (½in), then pin and stitch.

3 Lay the organza at the centre of the canvas and stitch around three sides, leaving the top edge open. Drop one leaf between the layers of fabric then carefully machine-sew around it, to enclose it in a pocket. Repeat until the organza panel has been filled with leaves in regular-sized pockets. Sew the top hem closed.

4 Screw the curtain-wire hooks in place. Pass the curtain wire through the channel at the top of the canvas panel and attach the hooks.

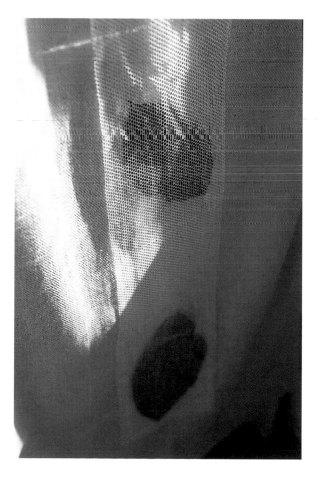

EQUIPMENT

MATERIALS AND

Tape measure and pencil
Cream cotton canvas
Scissors
Pins
Sewing machine and thread
Iron
Transparent organza fabric
Needle and thread
Dried leaves
Curtain wire and hooks

Customized cushion covers

Cushions are one of the best and quickest ways to finish off a room, instantly adding colour, shape and an air of comfort and relaxation. By painting a design on to cushion covers, Laurence has found a wonderful way of applying a strong theme right down to the smallest detail. When it comes to choosing a design, let your imagination run riot. Laurence was inspired by Aboriginal art taken from travel books, but any simple design would be just as effective.

EQUIPMENT

MATERIALS AND

Soft pencil

Images (from a copyright-free source)

Tracing paper

Cotton cushion cover (if making your own allow an extra 50cm (20in) of fabric for an envelope fastening)

Fabric paints: white, dark brown or black and your chosen colours

Artist's fine brush

Cushion pads

1 For each cushion, use a soft pencil and carefully copy the image directly on to the cushion cover, or trace it off the original. You can enlarge it if necessary by photocopying it to the appropriate size.

2 Having traced the design on to the fabric, paint around the outline with white fabric paint (use a dark colour if you are working on a pale background). Allow to dry.

3 Fill in the rest of the design with coloured fabric paints and allow to dry. Insert cushion pads.

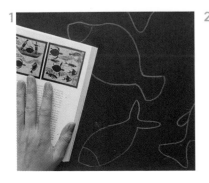

TOP TIP

Fabric paints are very versatile and can be used to great effect
on a number of different fabrics including velvet. Whatever
your chosen surface, a closely woven construction is
important to give a firm surface for the paint. You will not be
able to achieve as good a result using an open-weave fabric.

Lotus-leaf picture

Pictures really help to bring a room to life but finding, or affording, what you like can be difficult. Making your own collection is one solution. Here, Graham used dried leaves to make a striking picture, as they have a tactile quality that is in tune with the current trend towards textures. Of course, you don't have to use leaves, the advantage of making your own picture is that you can use materials that are suited to the style of your room.

1 Decide on the dimensions of your picture and cut a piece of hardboard to size. Measure the edges and cut lengths of timber to create the frame around the hardboard, either butt-joining or mitring the corners. Butt-joins will give a more rustic, handmade look than a mitred frame. Nail the frame to the hardboard so that it stands 2.5cm (1in) proud of the board. Paint the timber with dark oak wood stain and leave to dry.

2 When the frame is dry, line the inside with cream backing paper. Use glue or double-sided tape to secure the paper at each corner and in the middle. Mark the centre of the backing paper and glue the brown paper square on to it. Arrange the leaves and stick them in position.

3 Carefully cut the Perspex to size with the jigsaw, using the correct blade. It should be approximately 3mm (⅛in) smaller all around than the internal size of the picture. Lower the Perspex into place and hold it in

position with panel pins hammered into the centre of the frame edges at each side. Finally hang the picture using a picture-hanging kit.

EQUIPMENT

MATERIALS AND

Tape measure

Pencil

Hardboard

Jigsaw with timber-cutting blade; and Perspex-cutting blade

5 x 2.5cm (2 x 1in) timber

Saw

Mitre block (optional)

5cm (2in) nails

Hammer

Dark oak wood stain

13mm (½in) paintbrush

Cream backing paper

All-purpose glue or double-sided tape

Small square of brown paper

Dried lotus leaves (available from garden centres or florists)

Sheet of Perspex

Panel pins

Picture-hanging kit

1

2

3

TOP TIP

If you are investing time in making one picture, why not make two? Pictures work so much better in pairs or groups than as single items and hanging two gives them far more impact. Even if you use identical layouts, because leaves are natural objects each picture will maintain its own unique character.

Quilted dining-chair covers

Dining chairs can be expensive to buy. Graham's smart covers can turn mismatched scruffy ones into a pristine set, making a bold and cohesive impact with a chic and contemporary look. Choose chairs with a simple basic shape and fabric that will either match or complement the wall colours.

1 Rub down the chair with first medium-grade and then fine sandpaper to create a good 'key' for the paint. Wipe off any dust with a rag. Prime the chair with white acrylic primer, allow to dry, and then apply two coats of top colour, allowing the

paint to dry between coats. If using emulsion paint, apply a finishing layer of varnish and leave to dry.

2 Make a template for the cover by cutting newspaper to the size of the seat and back, including the length hanging down the back of the chair. If you are working with unquilted fabric and wadding, fold the cotton fabric in half and pin the template to it. With the tailor's chalk draw a line 5cm (2in) all around outside the template. Remove the template and cut around the chalked line through both layers of fabric. This will give you two pieces, one each for the front and the back of the cover.

3 Reuse the template to cut a single thickness of wadding, drawing around it with the chalk and cutting out as described in Step 2. Sandwich the wadding between the two pieces of cotton fabric and pin together around the edges.

4 To quilt the fabric yourself, pin the three layers together in a series of horizontal and vertical lines. Tack with long stitches and remove the pins. Working from the centre outwards, machine-stitch along the lines of

tacking. Remove the tacking stitches. If you have ready-quilted fabric, cut as a single thickness using the template and tailor's chalk, as described in Step 2.

5 Hold the cover against the chair and trim the edges neatly for a perfect fit. Sew the edges on the machine with a close zigzag stitch. Remove the pins.

6 Place the Velcro spots in position, one at each corner of the seat and one at each corner of the back, then press the cover down so that it is held firmly in place.

Painted banner

Printed fabrics, especially luxury ones like silk, can be wildly expensive, so Linda used fabric paints to add some pattern of her own.

EQUIPMENT

MATERIALS AND

Tape measure
Raw silk
Scissors
Velvet
Pins
Sewing machine and appropriate thread
Needle and thread
Pencil or tailor's chalk
Saucer or other round template
Fabric paint (3-D)
Hairdryer
Banner heading of your choice

1 Decide on the finished measurements of the banner, then deduct 8cm (3in) from each side for the velvet border. Cut the silk accordingly.

2 Cut a 20cm (8in) velvet strip for each of the four curtain edges. Pin to the silk using a 2.5cm (1in) seam allowance and machine-stitch into position. Check that the pile on all the velvet strips runs in the same direction, otherwise they could all seem to be different shades.

3 At the bottom of the banner, fold under the raw edge of the velvet border, then pin this folded edge to the fabric to cover the join with the silk. Mitre the corners, then fold and pin the velvet side-strips in the same way. Sew by hand and remove the pins. Mitre and hem the top strip.

4 Draw circles on to the silk using tailor's chalk or pencil, and a saucer as a template. Make a pencil cross in the centre of each circle. Knock the tip of the paint tube on a hard surface before use to get rid of air bubbles. Starting at the cross, hold the tube of paint at right angles to the fabric and squeeze out a pattern of spiralling dots. Dry the paint with the hairdryer.

5 Hang the banner with the heading of your choice, for example tie tops attached to curtain rings.

Timber candle holders

Candles instantly change the atmosphere of a room, casting a soft, flattering glow. Graham's distinctive candlesticks cost almost nothing to make.

1 Cut a suitable section of turned timber, with enough surface top and bottom to hold the candle, with the saw. If you use the legs from an old chair, for example, you will be able to make a matching pair of candlesticks. Sand to remove old paint and varnish.

2 Cut a block of timber or MDF for the base. This should be wider than the turned timber to give it a good anchor and stability. Glue and screw the block to the bottom of the timber.

3 At the other end, drill an aperture large enough to hold your candle. Sand the rough edges and then paint or varnish as you wish.

EQUIPMENT

MATERIALS AND

Old piece of turned wood, such as a chair leg or small table leg or a banister spindle

Saw

Sandpaper

Block of MDF or timber

Wood glue

Woodscrews

Drill

Screwdriver

Paint and/or varnish

Fruit-bowl light

The basis of Linda's unusual light fitting is a simple blue glass fruit-bowl, which looks beautiful with light streaming through it. When the light is switched on the copper-coloured sunray frame heightens the intense blue and casts fascinating shadows on the ceiling. Stylish lighting can be incredibly pricey, but this design will not cost a fortune.

1 Measure the diameter of the fruit bowl then, with a pencil, draw a slightly smaller circle on to the MDF. Draw another circle about 5cm (2in) outside this. Cut around both circles with the jigsaw to make a ring. The bowl should fit snugly within the ring, and should not protrude above the edge by more than a couple of millimetres.

2 Draw a circle on to the hardboard, about 1.25cm (½in) smaller than the diameter of the fruit bowl, and then draw another about 2.5cm (1in) outside it. Draw sun rays radiating out from the outer circle, keeping the width and length of the rays fairly even, and not too fine unless you are very confident with the jigsaw. Cut around the inner circle with the jigsaw, making a starting point in the centre of the circle. The circle will drop out. Then cut around the rays to leave a ring with spokes branching off it. The hardboard should sit on top of the MDF ring. There is no need to fix the components together. Spray both the MDF and hardboard pieces with copper paint.

3 Place the fruit bowl in the MDF ring and sit the hardboard sun on top. Mark three equally spaced dots on the MDF and fix one screw eye into each. Attach equal lengths of brass chain to the eyes and loop each chain over the brass ceiling hook. The light bulb should hang concealed just inside the fruit bowl. Finally, to avoid a stark central light, fit a dimmer switch so that you can give yourself a range of light levels.

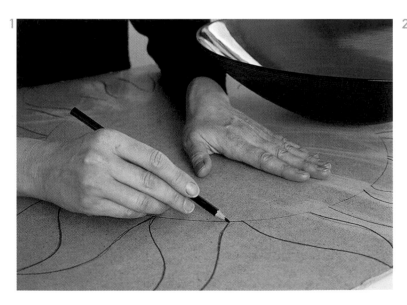

3

MATERIALS AND

Tape measure

Shallow blue glass fruit bowl

Pencil

Sheet of 9mm (⅜in) MDF

Round template

Jigsaw with timber-cutting blade

Hardboard

Copper paint spray

Screw eyes

Brass chain

Brass ceiling rose with central hook

TOP TIP

This light will work best in a room where strong overhead lighting is not required, or where there are alternative light sources for reading or close work. It is perfect for creating atmosphere in a dining room, or even for soft bedroom lighting.

All-purpose storage box

Homes today demand flexibility, and if an item of furniture can do more than one job then so much the better. These chunky storage boxes provide plenty of space for magazines, CDs or toys. They also have casters on the base for mobility and, with the addition of a cushion, can double as extra seating or a footrest.

1 Decide on the dimensions of your finished box and cut all four sides plus the top and bottom from MDF or plywood. A box 46cm (18in) wide, 41cm (16in) high and 36cm (14in) deep is a practical size, but you can suit your needs. The top should be the same size as the outer dimensions of the box while the bottom should be 2cm (¾in) smaller all around. Cut and fix vertical timber battens to the inside corners with glue and screws. The battens should stop some distance from what will be the bottom of the box. The space you leave must be exactly enough to accommodate the base panel and the height of the casters. The battens should be placed so that the base panel rests against them with its casters sticking out about 5mm (¼in) underneath.

2 Join the four sides of the box together with glue and screws, screwing through the vertical timber battens into the MDF panels. Cut four more horizontal battens to fit between the bottom ends of the vertical ones. These will support the base panel. Attach these to the sides with glue and screws.

3 Insert the base panel so that it rests against the horizontal battens and secure it in place with glue and screws.

4 Screw the four casters to the underside of the base panel, one in each corner, about 2.5cm (1in) away from the sides and so that they protrude by about 5mm (¼in).

5 Mark hand-holes on the sides of the box and cut them out with the jigsaw. These can be any shape so long as you can use them to open the lid.

6 Mark positions for the two hinges on the top back and on the lid. Check everything is lined up perfectly, then screw the hinges to the lid and then on to the box. It is now ready for the decoration of your choice.

EQUIPMENT

MATERIALS AND

- Tape measure
- Pencil
- 2cm (¾in) MDF or plywood: about one 1.2 x 1.2m (4 x 4ft) sheet per box
- Handsaw or jigsaw with timber-cutting blade
- 2.5 x 2.5cm (1 x 1in) timber batten: about 1.8m (6ft) per box
- Wood glue
- Drill with 3mm wood bit for pilot holes
- Screws
- Screwdriver; or screwdriver bit for drill
- Four casters and screws per box
- Two flush hinges and screws per box

1

2

3
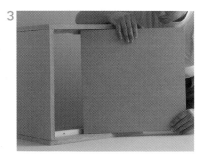

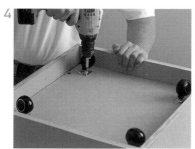

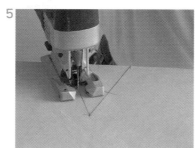

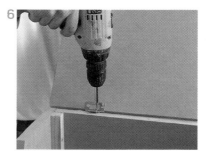

Custom-made bedhead

Good-looking bedheads are notoriously hard to find with most stores offering a stark choice of either Dralon or Victorian-style bedknobs. By making your own, as Linda has here, you can choose any fabric and work to any dimensions you want, so the finished result can complement your bedroom and is tailored to your needs.

1

2

3

1 Mark the measurements of your bedhead on the MDF. Cut out the MDF with the jigsaw and fix it to the wall. Use the drill and the 3mm wood bit to mark pilot holes in the wall. Then drill holes into the wall with the 6mm masonry bit, put in the wall plugs and screw the battens to the wall. Cut the foam to the same size as the MDF using a serrated knife. Spray contact adhesive on to the MDF and the wrong side of the foam. Once the adhesive is dry on both surfaces they can be bonded together.

2 Lay the fabric over the foam and secure it using a staple gun or hammer and tacks. Start at the centre of the long sides, then move to the centre of the short sides. Progress from the centre to each corner by degrees, keeping the fabric smooth as you work. Mitre each corner neatly.

3 Trim away the excess fabric with the scissors, taking care not to cut too close to the staples or tacks. Then prepare the wooden architrave, dowelling or bamboo to go around the edges and hide the staples. Paint or varnish as required first and allow to dry thoroughly. Mitre the corners with a mitre block and handsaw, sand any rough edges completely smooth and use panel adhesive to fix the wood in place. To increase the durability of the fabric, spray with upholstery protector.

EQUIPMENT

MATERIALS AND

Tape measure

Pencil

Sheet of 12mm (½in) MDF

Jigsaw with timber-cutting blade

Drill with 6mm masonry bit; 3mm wood bit for pilot holes

6mm wall plugs

Size 8 screws

Screwdriver

Piece of 5cm (2in) dense foam (fireproof)

Knife with serrated blade

Contact adhesive

Fabric to cover bedhead

Staple gun or hammer and tacks

Scissors

Wooden architrave, dowelling or bamboo sticks

Paint or varnish

Mitre block

Handsaw

Sandpaper

Panel adhesive

Upholstery protector

Copper pipe bed curtain rail

This budget idea creates the impression of a four-poster bed without using posts. It comes into its own in a room with a high ceiling, allowing space to make a dramatic column of fabric at each corner of the bed. The look is both timeless and elegant, but also seems to lower the ceiling, producing more intimate and pleasing proportions.

1 Measure the lengths of the sides, head and foot of your bed, and use a hacksaw or pipe-cutting tool to cut lengths of copper pipe to match. Using these lengths and 90-degree elbow joints, glue or solder together a frame the same size as your bed. Thread on the wardrobe rail brackets, and the curtain rings if required, before you secure the final corner.

2 You may need another pair of hands to help with this next stage. Hold the frame up against the ceiling directly over the bed, move each of the rail brackets to the same spot at each corner and use the 3mm wood bit to mark drill-hole positions for them.

3 Drill the marked holes with the 6mm masonry bit and insert cavity wall plugs or self-drill plasterboard fixings, which are specially designed for use in plasterboard. If you feel resistance from the drill, you may have hit a ceiling joist so use a conventional woodscrew to complete the task.

4 Screw the rail brackets into place using the wall plugs, then hang the curtains. Although the fixings are fairly robust you should avoid dragging too hard on the curtains.

EQUIPMENT

MATERIALS AND

Tape measure

Pencil

2cm (¾in) copper pipe: to fit the dimensions of the bed

Hacksaw or pipe-cutting tool

Four 2cm (¾in) copper elbow joints

Epoxy resin glue or solder and blowlamp

4 wardrobe rail brackets

Curtain rings (optional)

Drill with 6mm masonry bit; 3mm wood bit for pilot holes

Self-drill plasterboard fixing plugs or cavity wall plugs: one for each screw hole in the rail brackets

2cm (¾in) size 8 woodscrews (if not supplied with rail brackets)

Screwdriver; or screwdriver bit for drill

1
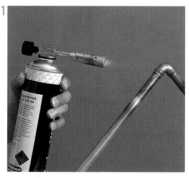

2
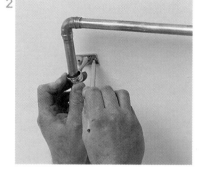

3

4

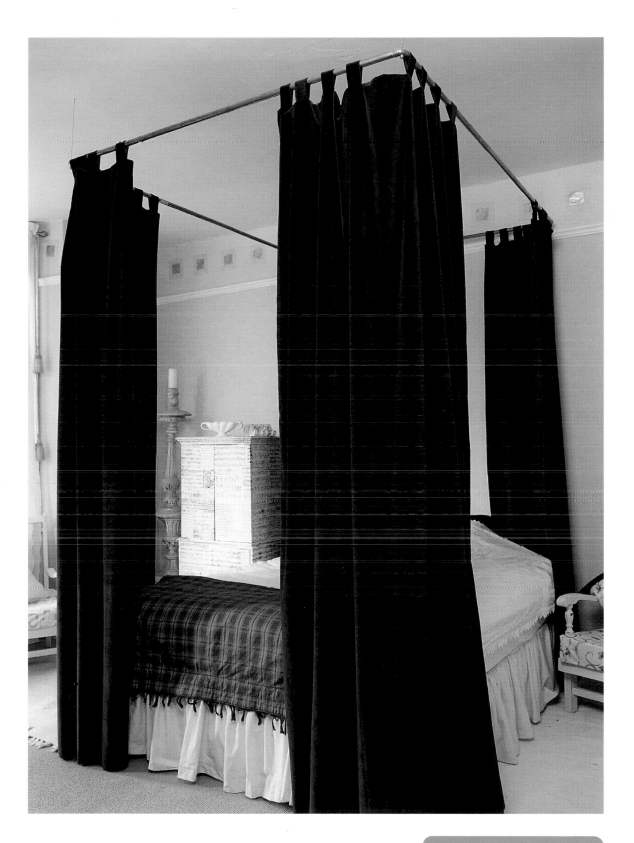

Mosaic firescreen

Laurence's idea for an attractive, colourful firescreen is useful for concealing an empty grate that could otherwise make a room feel unwelcoming. To get the best results, plan your design out carefully on paper first. Remember that the more intricate your design, the more difficult it will be to construct, so start with something quite simple.

1 Measure the opening for the mosaic in the firescreen frame and jigsaw a piece of MDF to fit. Apply a solution of half water, half PVA glue with the paintbrush to seal both sides and leave to dry for an hour. Draw the outlines for your mosaic on to the MDF (leave room round the edge for the panel to be screwed into the frame) and roughen the surface with the sharp teeth of a tenon saw.

2 Cut tile or ceramic pieces for the mosaic using tile nippers. Hold each tile between finger and thumb, place the cutting edge of the nippers over the edge and squeeze the nippers together. Fix the mosaic pieces in place with waterproof wood adhesive.

3 Fill the spaces between the tiles with waterproof grout, by spreading and working it over the surface with a rubber blade spreader until all the gaps are filled. Wipe away excess grout and leave to dry overnight before buffing with a clean cloth and screwing to the frame.

Ornate mirror frame

Mirrors are beautiful accessories and there is a huge range available in the shops. Linda decided, however, to make her own stunning mirror that would be totally unique.

1 Lie your mirror glass in the middle of the MDF or plywood sheet and draw around its edges. Use a paper template or work freehand to mark out the design of the frame around the outside of this area. Then mark a

second cutting line about 2.5cm (1in) inside the outline of the mirror. This will allow the frame a small overlap all the way around the glass, and leave space for the mirror clips to be fixed to the back. Make a drill hole with the 10mm wood bit then jigsaw out the inner and outer shape of the frame.

2 Sand all the edges and decorate the frame. It is much easier to do this before the glass goes in.

3 When decorated, secure the mirror glass in place by screwing a mirror clip to the back of the frame at each corner of the glass. Then add a couple of eyelet fixings to take the string or wire that will support the frame when hung. Check that the fixings are secure, then hang the mirror. Use either a screw attached to the wall with a wall plug, or a specialist fixing.

Play it safe

Unfortunately, the majority of accidents occur in the home and tackling DIY projects presents all sorts of opportunities for things to go wrong, with potentially painful or even tragic results. Always be aware that you are handling sharp and heavy instruments, electrical appliances, chemicals and rough or wet surfaces. You may also be working up ladders or in other less-than-straightforward locations. Here are some basic safety guidelines:

As a general rule, always read and follow the manufacturer's instructions for using any tools or materials.

Power tools

• Always check that you can switch off a tool, before switching on. Use a circuit-breaker between power tools and the socket. If there are problems, it will cut the current immediately.

• Be conscious of where your flex is trailing. Try to keep it behind you, and certainly well away from any cutting blades.
• Always fit the correct drill bit or cutting blade for the task you are attempting and do not try to use damaged or worn tools. If you find you have to force a tool into a material, stop work immediately because something is wrong.
• Start cutting only when the blade is at full speed. Never remove a drill, sander or power saw from the material until it has stopped completely.
• Wear protective goggles when using power saws, sanders and drills. Protect yourself from MDF dust by wearing a face mask when cutting and look out for children before you start.

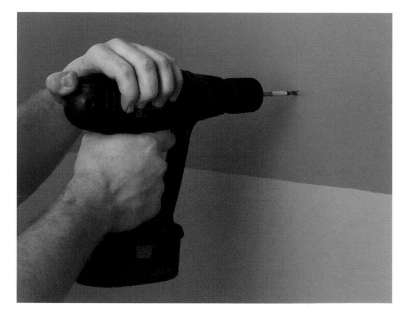

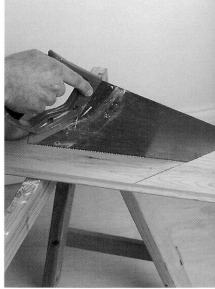

Tools

• Knife blades and chisels should always be worked away from your body, never towards you.

• Keep blades and chisels sharp. They will work more efficiently and be less likely to slip and cut you.

Electricity

• Always consult a qualified electrician before altering or installing lighting or any other electrical equipment, and get newly fitted equipment checked by a professional.

• Never allow flexes to trail across floors or under carpets. They should be stapled in position along skirtings, walls or ceilings.

• In an emergency switch off electricity by operating the main switch on the consumer unit.

• Only buy equipment displaying the kitemark (the British Standards mark of safety).

• Never drill near light switches or sockets. Buy a small detector device for checking whether cables or pipes are hidden behind plaster.

Ladders

• Choose a ladder that gives access to the highest point you wish to reach.

• Where a stepladder is not high enough, use a combination ladder that will convert into a stepladder.

• Never rest a ladder against glass.

• Use an S-shaped hook to hang a paint kettle or container from a ladder when working.

• Under certain circumstances, where ceilings are very high, it is safer to hire a scaffolding tower with decking boards fitted across rather than use inadequate ladders. Your safety is worth the extra outlay.

Paints and solvents

• Wear goggles to protect your eyes from flying particles of paint, dust and rust when preparing areas for painting.

• Keep the room in which you are painting well ventilated and leave doors and windows open for as long as possible afterwards. When using strippers, spray paints, glues and varnishes try to work outside and always wear a protective face mask.

• Protect your hands from chemicals, strippers and varnishes with thick rubber gloves. If stripper gets on to your skin wash it off immediately with cold water. Although water-based products are less hazardous, it makes sense to also wear gloves for handling them.

• Keep pets and children away when you are working with chemicals and paints. Remember, these are poisonous, often flammable materials that should be carefully stored out of reach and away from heat. Replace lids firmly and never transfer any chemical substance into an alternative container where it could be mistaken for food or drink.

Useful addresses

Art and craft equipment

ATLANTIS EUROPEAN LIMITED, 7–9 Plumbers Row, London E1 1EQ. Tel: 020 7377 8855

COLART FINE ART AND GRAPHICS LIMITED (Liquitex) White Friars Avenue, Harrow, Middlesex HA3 5RH. Tel: 0800 212822

DALER ROWNEY ARTISTS MATERIALS, PO Box 10, Bracknell, Berkshire RG12 8ST. Tel: 01344 424621

DYLON INTERNATIONAL LIMITED (dyes), Worsely Bridge Road, Lower Sydenham, London SE26 5HD. Tel: 020 8663 4296

HOBBYCRAFT, 7 Enterprise Way, Aviation Park, Bournemouth International Airport, Christchurch, Dorset BH23 6HG. Tel: 08000 272387

HOMECRAFTS DIRECT, PO Box 38, Leicester LE1 9BU. Tel: 0116 2513139

THE MOSAIC WORKSHOP, Unit B, 443–9 Holloway Road, London N7 6LJ. Tel: 020 7263 2997 (mail order service and courses)

PAPERCHASE, 213 Tottenham Court Road, London W1T 9PS. Tel: 020 7467 6200

PEBEO (paint and craft paint). Tel: 02392 701144 (for nearest stockist)

RUSSELL AND CHAPPLE (artists materials), 68 Drury Lane, London WC2B 5SP. Tel: 020 7836 7521

THE STENCIL STORE GROUP PLC, 20/21 Heronsgate Road, Chorleywood, Hertfordshire WD3 5BN. Tel: 01923 285577/88

ALEC TIRANTI (model makers' tools and materials), 27 Warren Street, London W1T 5NB. Tel: 020 7636 8565

Building and DIY materials

ARTEX RAWLPLUG LIMITED (wall plugs and tile tools) Skibo Drive, Thornliebank Industrial Estate, Glasgow G46 8JR. Tel: 0141 638 7961

BLACK AND DECKER, Tel: 01753 511234 (information line for local stockists)

BMJ POWER (Black and Decker stockists), Unit 15, Shield Drive, West Cross Centre, Great West Road, Brentford TW8 9EX. Tel: 0345 230230

BOSCH LIMITED, PO Box 98, Broadwater Park, Denham, Middlesex UB9 5HJ. Tel: 01895 838743

BUCK AND RYAN, 101 Tottenham Court Road, London W1T 4DY. Tel: 020 7636 7475

DRAPER TOOLS LIMITED, Hursley Road, Chandler's Ford Eastleigh, Hants SO53 1YF. Tel: 02380 266355

NATURAL FLOORING DIRECT, 46 Webs Road, Battersea, London SW11 6SF. Tel: 0800 454721

PLASPLUGS LIMITED (wall plugs and tile tools), Wetmore Road Burton-on-Trent, Staffordshire DE14 1SD. Tel: 01283 530303

REJECT TILE SHOP, 178 Wandsworth Bridge Road, Fulham, London SW6 2UQ. Tel: 020 7731 6098

SALVO, PO Box 333, Cornhill-on-Tweed, Northumberland TD12 4YJ. Tel: 01890 820333

SILVERMANS (TIMBER), Unit 3, Elstree Distribution Park Elstree Way, Borehamwood, Hertfordshire WD6 1RU. Tel: 020 8238 6930

SOLOPARK (reclaimed building materials/period architectural items), Station Road, Nr Pampisford, Cambridgeshire CB2 4HB. Tel: 01223 834663

STANLEY TOOLS, Woodside, Sheffield S3 9PD. Tel: 0114 276 8888

THE TARMAC GROUP, PO Box 8, Millfield Road, Ettingshall, Wolverhampton WV4 6JP. Tel: 01902 353522

TOPP'S TILES, Unit D, Mortimer Road Industrial Estate, Narbrough, Leicester LE9 5GA. Tel: 0800 7836262

TRAVIS PERKINS, Lodge Way House, Harlestone Road, Northampton NN5 7UG. Tel: 01604 752424

WALCOT RECLAMATION, The Depot, Riverside Business Park, Lower Bristol Road, Bath BA2 3DW. Tel: 01225 335532

GLYN WEBB (home improvements), Old Derby House, Derker Street, Oldham OL1 3XF. Tel: 0161 6214500

WICKES BUILDING SUPPLIES LIMITED, 120-138 Station Road, Harrow, Middlesex HA1 2QB. Tel: 0500 300328

Paints and decorating equipment

BRATS, 281 Kings Road, London SW3 5EW. Tel: 020 7351 7674

CROWN PAINTS, Crown House, PO Box 37, Hollins Road, Darwin, Lancashire BB3 0BG. Tel: 01254 704951

CUPRINOL LTD (paints), Adderwell Road, Frome, Somerset BA11 1NL. Tel: 01373 475000

THE DECORATING CENTRE.COM, 9 Ainsty Road, Wetherby, West Yorkshire LS22 7QN. Tel: 01937 580980

DULUX, ICI Paints, Wexham Road, Slough, Berkshire SL2 5DS. Tel: 01753 550555

FARROW & BALL, Uddens Trading Estate, Wimborne, Dorset BH21 7NL. Tel: 01202 876141

HAMMERITE PRODUCTS LTD, Prudhoe, Northumberland NE42 6LP. Tel: 01661 830000

KALON DECORATIVE PRODUCTS (produce Johnstones and Leyland paints), Huddersfield Road, Burstall, Batley, West Yorkshire WF17 9XA. Tel: 01924 3544703

LIBERON LIMITED (wax, wood care and coloured stains) Learoyd Road, Mountfield Industrial Estate, New Romney, Kent TN28 8XU. Tel: 01797 367555

RAY MUNN, 861–863 Fulham Road, London SW6 5HP. Tel: 020 7736 9876

PAINTWORKS, 5 Elgin Crescent, Notting Hill, London W11 2JA. Tel: 020 7792 8012

PAPERS AND PAINTS (craft materials and paint), 4 Park Walk, London SW10 0AD. Tel: 020 7352 8626 (mail order service)

PLASCON INTERNATIONAL LIMITED, Brewery House, High Street, Twyford, Winchester SO21 1RG. Tel: 01962 717001/2

PLASTI-KOTE (spray paints and varnishes), PO Box 867, Pampisford, Cambridge CB2 4XP. Tel: 01223 836400

POLYVINE, 1 Marybrook Street, Rockhampton, Berkeley, Gloucestershire GL13 9AA. Tel: 0870 7873710

RONSEAL LTD (paints and varnishes), Thorncliff Park, Chapeltown, Sheffield S35 2YP. Tel: 0114 2467171

SANDERSON (paints), Sanderson House, Oxford Road, Denham, Middlesex UB9 4DX. Tel: 01895 251288

GEORGE WEIL FIBRE CRAFTS (silk and silk paints, glass and ceramic paints), Old Portsmouth Road, Peasmarsh, Guildford, Surrey GU3 1LZ. Tel: 01483 565800

Textiles

ALMA LEATHER (leather skin/interiors), Unit D, 12–14 Great Torex Street, London E1 5NF. Tel: 020 7375 0343

BARNETT & LAWSON TRIMMINGS, 16/17 Little Portland Street, London W1W 8NF. Tel: 020 7636 8591 (Mail order service)

BOROVICKS, 16 Berwick Street, London W1F 0HP. Tel: 020 7437 2180

DALSTON MILLS, 69–73 Ridley Road, Dalston, Hackney, London E8 2NP. Tel: 020 7249 4129

GANESHA (textiles/fairtrade supplier), 3 Gabriels Wharf, 56 Upper Ground, London SE1 9PP. Tel: 020 7928 3444

MALABAR, 31/33 The South Bank Business Centre, Ponton Road, London SW8 5BL. Tel: 020 7501 4200

NATURAL FABRIC COMPANY, Wessex Place, 127 High Street, Hungerford, Berkshire RG17 0DL. Tel: 01488 684002

NICE IRMA'S, Unit 2, Finchley Industrial Centre, 879 High Road, London N12 8QA. Tel: 020 8343 7610 (mail order service)

PENTONVILLE RUBBER PRODUCTS (foam cubes, upholstery foam), 104–106 Pentonville Road, London N1 9JB. Tel: 020 7837 4582

RUFFLETTE LTD (curtains, headings and hooks), Sharston Road, Manchester M22 4TH. Tel: 0161 998 1811

SOMERSBY TEXTILES, 55 Fashion Street, London E1 6TX. Tel: 020 7247 8008

WOLFIN TEXTILES, 64 Great Titchfield Street, London W1W 7QH. Tel: 020 7636 4949

General

ARGOS. Tel: 0870 600 3030 (for nearest store and enquiries)

B&Q PLC, Portswood House, I Hampshire Corporate Park, Chandlers Ford, Eastley, Hampshire SO53 3YX. Tel: 02380 256256

BHS, Marylebone House, 129/137 Marylebone Road, London NW1 5QD. Tel: 020 7262 3288

CARGO HOME STORES, Thame Park Industrial Estate, Thame, Oxfordshire OX9 3HD. Tel: 0870 2410304

FOCUS DO IT ALL (DIY), Gawsworth House, Westmere Drive, Crewe, Cheshire CW1 6XB. Tel: 0800 436436

GREAT MILLS HEAD OFFICE, Paulton, Bristol BS39 7SX. Tel: 01761 416034

HABITAT. Tel: 0845 6010740 (for nearest store and customer enquiries)

HOMEBASE, Beddington House, Wallington, Surrey SM6 OHB. Tel: 0870 9008098

HSS (hire), 25 Willow Lane, Mitcham, Surrey CR4 4TS. Tel: 0161 839 5238

IKEA, 2 Drury Way, North Circular Road, London NW10 0TH. Tel: 020 8208 5600 (for nearest store)

IMPROMILL, 142 Holloway Road, London N7 8DD. Tel: 020 7607 7461

LAKELAND PLASTICS, Alexandra Buildings, Windermere, Cumbria LA23 1BQ. Tel: 01539 488100 (mail order service)

JOHN LEWIS PLC, 171 Victoria Street, London SW1E 5NN. Tel: 020 7828 1000 (for nearest store and customer enquiries)

THE PIER, 91/95 King's Road, London SW3 4PA. Enquiry line: 020 7814 5020 (for nearest store)

SELFRIDGES & CO, 400 Oxford Street, London W1A 1AB. Tel: 020 7629 1234

TESCO HOME. Tel: 0800 505555 (for nearest store)

Miscellaneous

ALMO OFFICE (ACETATE SHEETS), Unit 16, Bermondsey, Trading Estate, Rotherhythe New Road, London SE16 3LL. Tel: 020 7635 3500

JALI LIMITED, Albion Works, Church Lane, Barham, Canterbury, Kent CT4 6QS. Tel: 01277 831710 (mail order service)

LASSCO (salvage yards), St Michael's Church, Mark Street, Off Paul Street, London EC2A 4ER. Tel: 020 7739 0448

METAL SUPERMARKET (basic metal materials), Unit 11, Hanover West Trading Estate, 161 Acton Lane, Park Royal, London NW10 7NB. Tel: 020 8961 1414

QVS (electrical equipment, including light fittings), 168 Brighton Road, Coulsdon, Surrey CR5 2NE. Tel: 0800 801733

THATCH INTERNATIONAL (rolls of willow screening), Unit 20, Stonefield Park, Chilbolton, Hampshire SO20 6BL. Tel: 01264 861319

ANDY THORNTON ARCHITECTURAL ANTIQUES LIMITED, Victoria Mills, Stainland Road, Greetland, Halifax, West Yorkshire HX4 8AD. Tel: 01422 377314

3M (wide range of products including various adhesives). Tel: 08705 360036 (for specific product queries and local suppliers)

Measurement conversion chart

If you get stuck over measurements and want a handy rule of thumb for quick comparisons, the following rough conversions should help. 10ft is just over 3 metres, so 1 metre is roughly 3ft 3in. For smaller measurements, imagine a standard 12in ruler and remember that it's fairly close to 30cm. For greater precision, the following should help:

To convert imperial to metric:

Yards to metres - multiply by 0.9144

Feet to metres - multiply by 0.3048

Inches to centimetres - multiply by 2.54

Inches to millimetres - multiply by 25.4

Square yards to square metres - multiply by 0.8361

Square feet to square metres - multiply by 0.0929

To convert metric to imperial:

Metres to yards - divide by 0.9144

Metres to feet - divide by 0.3048

Centimetres to inches - divide by 2.54

Millimetres to inches - divide by 25.4

Square metres to square yards - divide by 0.8361

Square metres to square feet - divide by 0.0929

Index

Page numbers in *italic* refer to illustrations.

Picture credits

BBC Worldwide would like to thank the following for providing photographs and permission to reproduce copyright material. While every effort has been made to trace and acknowledge all copyright holders, we would like to apologize should there have been any errors or omissions.

© **BBC Worldwide:** 66, 122(l); (Paul Bricknell), 4(l), 122(r), 140, 141, 148–9, 152–7, 160–1, 170–1, 176–9, 182–7, 190–3, 200–5, 208–17, 222–3, 240–1, 244–5, 247–8, 249(l), 252; (Robin Matthews), 4(r), 5(r), 15(b), 17, 66(b), 70, 72–3, 74(t), 142, 143, 151, 162–3, 166–7, 174, 186–8, 194–6, 199(t), 207, 220, 224, 226, 228–30, 232, 234–7, 239(t), 242; (Ed Reeve) 3, 5(l), 12, 18, 22–30, 34–9, 41–51, 52–4, 56, 58–60, 63–4, 65(r), 74(b), 76, 78(r), 79(b), 126–37, 144–6, 158–9, 172–3, 189, 197–8, 199(b), 218–19, 221, 225, 227(r), 231, 233, 238, 239(b), 243(t), 249(r); (Shona Wood), 13, 14, 15(t), 16, 71, 86–97, 104–21, 138, 150, 164–5, 168–9, 175, 180–1, 246.
BBC Good Homes Magazine (Steve Dalton) 21, 31; (Georgia Glynn Smith) 62, 77(r); (Neil Marsh) 19; (Robin Matthews) 55, 68, 80–5, 98–103; (Nadia McKenzie) 20, 75(r); (Tom Leighton) 40, 78(l); (Lu Symonds) 61; (Simon Whitmore) 79(t); (Mark Williams) 75(l); (Tim Young) 69.
BBC Homes & Antiques Magazine 57, 65(l), 77(l).